GLIMPSES *of* MEDFORD

GLIMPSES of
MEDFORD

Selections from the Historical Register

EDITED BY BARBARA KERR

Charleston ‖ London

History
PRESS

Published by The History Press
Charleston, SC 29403
www.historypress.net

Front Cover: An early photo of High Street looking east.

Back Cover: Members of the Medford Historical Society laying the cornerstone of the Governors Avenue Building in 1916.

First published 2007

Manufactured in the United Kingdom

ISBN 978.1.59629.231.4

Library of Congress CIP data applied for.

Notice: The information in this book is true and complete to the best of our knowledge. It is offered without guarantee on the part of the author or The History Press. The author and The History Press disclaim all liability in connection with the use of this book.

For Medford historians—past, present and future.

"There is nothing lost when we know where it is."

Medford Historical Register vol. 22, 1919

CONTENTS

Contents

ACKNOWLEDGEMENTS

Condensing forty-two volumes into a single one was a daunting task. The majority of the history recorded in the *Register* concerns Medford prior to 1900. For the sake of simplicity, the chapters in this book reflect that time period. Many of the articles are unabridged, but others have been edited so that as many selections as possible could be included. I think the selections reflect the best work of Medford's past historians, and I thank them for their accomplishments.

Copies of the complete *Medford Historical Register* can be found at the Medford Public Library and the Medford Historical Society. Some volumes are also available online through the Perseus Digital Library at Tufts University. The photographs in this book can be found in the collections of both the Medford Public Library and the Medford Historical Society.

I would like to thank the following: John Lonergan, Michael Bradford and Ryan Hayward of the Medford Historical Society; Brian Boutilier of the Medford Public Library; Gregory Crane and Alison Jones of the Perseus Project at Tufts University; Tony Mattera for his technical support; and my cats, Koko and Archie, who did not sit on the historical photographs in spite of great temptation.

INTRODUCTION

This is a book of Medford history written by Medford historians. In the 1890s, Medford, Massachusetts, was a thriving place. The gradual growth that began when the railroad came through town in the 1830s exploded after the Civil War, and the population grew from 4,800 citizens in 1860 to 18,000 by the turn of the century. It must have been a very exciting time to live, a time when it seemed that everything was new.

The history of Medford after the Civil War is a history of change. As new people moved to the town, they demanded new things—houses, businesses, city services. New churches and schools sprang up in every neighborhood, and city departments expanded to meet the needs of the population. Everything was new, from the paved streets to the sewer pipes to the institutions that were created to answer the educational and entertainment demands of the growing population.

One of these institutions was the Medford Historical Society, which was founded in 1896 by a group of 132 civic-minded residents. The founding of the society may very well have been a reaction to the constant change of the Victorian era. In the first issue of the *Medford Historical Register*, an author recording the society founding remarked that "it is a cause for regret that such a society had not been organized many years ago, as doubtless with the breaking up of old families year by year, much of the antiquarian interest and value has been scattered."[1] The object of the society was "to collect, preserve and disseminate the local and general history of Medford and the genealogy of Medford families."[2] To this end, the society settled into the house that had been the birthplace of abolitionist Lydia Maria

Child and remained there until 1916, when the current society building was constructed on Governors Avenue.

Within its first year the historical society gave Medford a great and lasting gift in the form of the *Medford Historical Register*. The *Register* was published four times a year from 1898 to 1940. The publication was a compendium of research articles, images, biographies, texts of papers and speeches, reminiscences, reproductions of documents and town records, with the occasional poem or play thrown in for variety. Much of what we know about Medford history comes from the *Register*. The early members of the society could not have done better in their efforts to preserve Medford's history.

The *Register* investigates all things Medford. Although the authors were amateur historians, their research is thorough and the stories they tell are fascinating and very detailed. Some of the pieces are exhaustive explorations of a subject, and some are short commentaries. There are genealogies of families and the histories of businesses. There are invaluable reminiscences by Medford residents who had been born in the nineteenth century and remembered the town before the great changes began. There are articles about Medford's founding and the Revolutionary War, the shipbuilding industry and Medford's famous people and noteworthy events. There are accounts of the railroad and streetcars and the Middlesex Canal, and many, many articles about houses, bridges, brooks and other works of man and nature.

There are some surprising omissions from the *Register*, however. Medford's brick-making industry is not mentioned at all, and there is surprisingly little written about Medford rum. There are some references to distilling, but there is no comprehensive work on the industry in any of the volumes. It would be interesting to know the story behind the lack of a story about Medford rum, but sadly, we will never find that history in the *Register*.

What you will find in its pages is the history of a town with a river running through the middle of it. Keep the river in mind as you read the selections in this book. In this day and age we don't think about the Mystic River very often, but in Medford's past the river was the origin and the lifeblood of the town. In these chapters you will see it as the goal of explorers, the source of industry, a place of beauty and recreation and, on one particular day in 1842, the place where a Mr. Russell of Medford caught 107,000 fish in one net. (See chapter five.) The Medford and the Mystic River of those long-ago days no longer exists anywhere but in the history books. Fortunately for us, the Medford Historical Society wrote those history books and you will find all the stories of long-ago Medford in their words. It is a fascinating place and you will be glad you came.

[1] *Medford Historical Register,* Medford Historical Society, 1898, 11.
[2] Ibid.

Chapter 1

EARLY DAYS

WHY MYSTIC?
Moses Whitcher Mann

The earliest mention of our river is said to have been made by some of the Plymouth Pilgrims in September 1621, who said, "Within this bay the salvages say there are two rivers: one whereof we saw having a fair entrance but we had no time to discover it."

Later comes Johnson, who in his _Wonder-Working Providence_ in describing Charlestown tells of "the pleasant and navigable river of Mistick," using the name that Governor Winthrop wrote in his diary under the date of June 17, 1630. "We went up Mystick River about six miles."

Dudley, in his letter to the Countess of Lincoln on March 28, 1631, tells of settlers at Watertown, on the Charles River, and "some of us upon Mistick, which we called Meadford." And again Winthrop tells, "The Governor and others went over Mistic River at Medford two or three miles among the rocks to a very great pond which they called Spot Pond."

Even a cursory glance at the early maps, and especially at one of latest survey on which the ancient lines are drawn, will show the fitness of the aboriginal names, for of the two rivers the "salvages" told the Pilgrim scouts of, one was the long river and the other the great wave- and wind-driven river of Boston Bay.

But perhaps someone asks, "Why Mystic River?" We reply that the river has nothing mystical or mysterious, and the name as spelled, Mystic, is a misnomer. It has come to be thus commonly spelled because of the identical sound of the letters "i" and "y," and the dropping of the "k," which in time was superfluous to the "c," which the English had introduced.

Where did Winthrop's six-mile journey begin? Naturally, we reply, at the mouth of the river, the "fair entrance" of the Pilgrim narrative, where is now the Chelsea bridge. There has been a lot said and written about Winthrop being the founder of Medford—well enough in a way, as he was the colonial governor—but the earliest Medford was Cradock's farm, and lay entirely on the opposite side of the river from Winthrop's. It has been written that "the first exploration of the river carried probably as far as Medford lines," and that "the English eyes in that boat were the first eyes of settlers that looked upon the fields on which we now live."

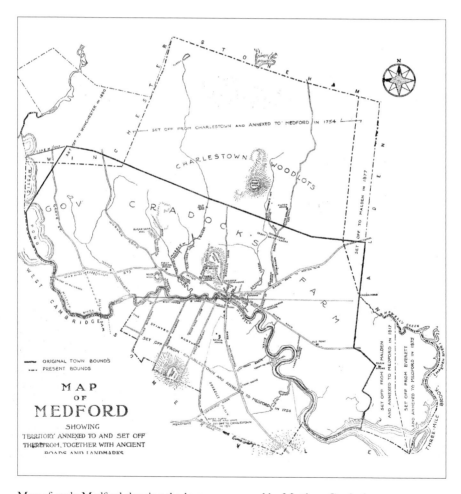

Map of early Medford showing the large area owned by Matthew Cradock.

We know not how those six miles were computed, and doubt whether Winthrop's company reached the farther Medford lines, or even Mistick pond or the Indian "weare." The sinuous course of the river (that doubled up at Labor-in-vain, and thrice again alongside Winthrop's farm), and his failure to mention the ponds, makes it improbable. But six miles would take the voyagers by the Ten-hills Farm and the ford and to the scarred promontory of Rock Hill. From the ford onward, the sylvan scene must have been enchanting, as the Medford Pasture Hill with its wooded slopes rose abruptly from the plain beside Gravelly Brook, but more gently from the river. Then came the brooks before and beyond Rock Hill, those later to be known as Meeting-house and Whitmore, and then the long encircling reach of the river to the Indian weare and fording place.

Surely the Cradock farm was beautiful for situation, "four miles along the river and a mile back in all places." Winthrop's farm was in Charlestown (he was not a Medfordite at all), and extended from just below the ford downstream below the slope of Winter Hill. There was a lot of marshland even in the Ten-hills Farm. But it was on the lower end of this farm that the *Blessing of the Bay* was built.

The Cradock House, built in 1634. Also known as the Peter Tufts House and the Old Fort. Photographed in 1891.

The governor seems to have liked the old Indian name of Missi-tuk or Mistuck, Mistick, Misticke or Mystycke, as he tells of his house and farm at Mistick in a perfectly natural way and with no mysticism or mystery at all. But in 1754 the little four-mile town of Meadford needed more room, and ancient Charlestown was too encircling, so the portion of Winthrop's farm and some more of Charlestown from the top of Winter Hill following some pasture lines over Walnut-tree Hill to the river, a triangular plat next to Woburn and the Charlestown wood lots next to Malden were annexed to Medford.

While this placed the entire width of the river, with two tributaries, in Medford for over two miles, Charlestown still had another mile, with its cow pastures and the "line field," through which flowed the Menotomy River, below the Indian weare and fording place. Fifty years later she surrendered the line field to the new town of West Cambridge, and a century later all her remaining territory outside the peninsula became the town of Somerville.

Along with and following the governor in those early years came some eighteen hundred settlers, some of whom found homes across the river where now is Wellington, and at Mystic-side or Maiden. To accommodate these a ferry was established, and the Missi-tuk began to be a highway, and later began to be utilized for power when mills were erected. Next came the bridge built near the ford, which, during the shipbuilding period, was reconstructed with a draw, and finally succeeded by the present double-arched granite structure. Next was built the Wear Bridge, and these two continued to be the only bridges until the Maiden Bridge was built at the Penny-ferry in Charlestown.

The colony and province days had been a quarter-century gone ere the Mistick was bridged again, this time by a more massive structure, strong enough to carry not a highway, but a waterway, with its superincumbent weight, the aqueduct of the Middlesex Canal. This was in 1802. Thirty-two years more and the canal was to have a rival, and Lowell Railroad Bridge was built nearby, the Winthrop Bridge in 1855 and the Usher Bridge in 1857. In 1863 the Charlestown Water-works Bridge, and in 1873 the Canal Bridge on the old aqueduct piers, connected West Medford with Somerville territory, and another at Auburn Street the same year. Meanwhile the Middlesex Avenue Bridge, with a draw, had been erected, and in earlier years (downstream, and not in Medford bounds) Chelsea Bridge and those of the Eastern and Boston & Maine Railroads. In recent years the Canal, Armory, Auburn Street Parkway and Metropolitan Pipe Bridges, and just now the Boston Elevated to Everett, complete the list of fourteen now in use and two discontinued and removed.

The canal aqueduct over the upper Mystic navigated by the steamboat *Merrimack*, circa 1818.

The granite Cradock Bridge photographed on its completion in 1880. Until 1879, the bridge was a wooden drawbridge that allowed the passage of ships.

GLIMPSES OF MEDFORD: SELECTIONS FROM THE HISTORICAL REGISTER

From the hill slopes of forty-five square miles the rains and melting snows reach our river and swell its current above the ancient ford. The ever-recurring tides ebbed and flowed therein until, in 1908, in the interest of public welfare, engineering skill erected a barrier that said, "Thus far but no farther." Cradock Bridge—its extension, the lock with its electrically operated gates, the dam with its automatic tidal valves and the four hundred feet of over-fall—is in marked contrast with the earliest structure, the bone of contention of those early days. Without these the beautiful parkway would have been impossible.

Along the river's banks have been scenes of activity in days now long gone, for

> *Here rested the noble ships,*
> *Keel, frame and towering spar,*
> *And where the horizon dips,*
> *They sailed and vanished afar.*

Little is known of the final fate of 567 of these ships. Upstream "the rent wharf wasted away" until the steam dredge removed islands, deepened the channel, eliminated some of the serpentine courses and bordered the stream with the valley parkway. Beneath the river cross water mains and sewers, while on its surface numerous pleasure craft make their way or find moorings. We have heard of no Mystic submarines in the waters, but winged ships of the air have flown up its course and over its tributary, Menotomy.

After the Civil War the project was broached of dredging and widening our river and making a storage basin of the lower lake for the monitors of the navy. But a few years before there had been built the dam at the "Partings," and the upper lake had become the Charlestown water supply.

Another project that failed was, in 1876, the Mystic Valley railroad that began to fill an embankment requiring a bridge across the old course of the Aberjona at the upper end of the lake. This, the upper reach of the Mystic (and sometimes called Symmes' River), had been crossed by the long wooden aqueduct of the canal in 1802, replaced by the substantial stone structure of 1827 and removed in 1865, as was also the Symmes dam and water power the same year.

And now we come back to our caption query: why Mystic? The answer: Mystic it is not, except by common usage. Missi-tuk, the Indians called it. The early settlers adopted the Indian name, spelling it various ways, and later, almost discarding it, called it often Medford River and Medford Pond or Ponds, and latterly Mystic, which, we repeat, is a misnomer.

Originally published in vol. 21, 1918.

Indians in Medford
Ruth Dame Coolidge

Long before Matthew Cradock had conceived the idea of a plantation on the Mystic River, the Indians had made their home beside the Missituk lakes. These Indians in Medford belonged to the tribe of the Massachusett, which inhabited practically all the east central part of the state. Early explorers tell us that the country was more or less open, that there were many cleared fields and that the underbrush in the forests was burned annually to open the woods for hunting, while Indian trails ran between the various Indian villages and to hunting or fishing grounds. Shortly before the arrival of the Pilgrims the Massachusett had been decimated by a terrible plague and many of the villages were deserted.

The larger part of Middlesex and Essex Counties was under the rule of an Indian sachem, Nanepashemit by name, who came to Medford from Lynn about 1615 and had the outpost on Rock Hill overlooking the river. He was killed in 1619, perhaps by his hereditary enemies, the Tarratines, who often came down from the north in the autumn, swept up the river in their canoes and destroyed or pillaged the crops of corn. Nanepashemit was succeeded by his wife, the "Squa Sachem," with her second mate, the sorcerer Webcowit, while the sachem's three sons became the sagamores, George of Salem, James of Lynn and John of Medford.

In Indian days there were doubtless trails between these various villages. There was a trail, too, from Charlestown to the famous fish weirs where the lakes narrow into the river—substantially along the lines of Main and High Streets of today—and another probably along Grove Street toward the hunting grounds in Woburn. Our early roads doubtless followed Indian trails. Numerous Indian relics, still found occasionally under the plough, and the graves of Indians near Sagamore Avenue in West Medford and on the hillside not far from the old pumping station, mutely attest to the presence of large Indian villages. The great run of alewives and smelts in the spring also brought the surrounding country Indians, who erected temporary fishing camps near the "Rock" meadows. Their houses were of two types. The more permanent ones were large and oblong, made of closely planted poles bent over like a grape arbor and carefully shingled with pieces of flattened bark. The temporary ones were round, with frameworks of poles covered with removable mats of woven cattails or grass, but not conical like the teepees of the western Indians, which could be rolled up and dragged from one place to another. Inside the houses were long bunk-like platforms and a full equipment of baskets, wood utensils and clay pots, though the French traders along shore early supplied Indians near the coast with iron or copper kettles.

Early Days

In September 1621, a party of Pilgrims from Plymouth explored Massachusetts Bay, and Medford historians have always believed that the account of this trip recounted in Mourt's *Relation* pointed clearly to Medford. These explorers found the wigwam of Nanepashemit on Rock Hill, a stockaded village some way beyond additionally protected by a moat and bridge, with a house within the stockade "wherein being dead he lay buryd." Beyond, on a gently sloping hill with great oak trees, there was another wigwam in which Nanepashemit had been killed. The Pilgrims followed the Indians and finally overtook the women of the tribe. With these they made peace, and their guests partook of a dinner, probably a porridge of beans, corn and dried alewives. The men were away, and the Squa Sachem too, with whom they had wished to make a treaty, was "not here," as the interpreter said, but they traded skins with the squaws and returned to Plymouth, wishing they had "been ther seated."

In later days Sagamore John was friendly toward Cradock's settlers, and indeed Matthew Cradock was very explicit in his directions to his men not to molest the Indians and to recompense them for their land. When Sagamore John died he regretted that he had not worshipped the white man's god, and he left his son as a ward to the Reverend John Wilson, who owned what is now Wellington, to be brought up as his ward. A deed granting land to Winthrop, but reserving the use of the weirs to the Indians, was signed in 1639 with the crosses of the Squa Sachem and Webcowit. Early maps show the lodges of Sagamore John on the south side of the river where it is joined by Alewife Brook. Gradually the Indians withdrew, though the remnants of the tribe made their home in Turkey Swamp, now Winchester Reservoir, and old accounts show that the Indians occasionally worked for the white men. The last Medford Indian was Hannah Shiner, who, under the civilizing influence of Medford rum, was drowned in the early nineteenth century.

The only tangible reminders of the presence of the Indians today are the relics in the collection of the Medford Historical Society and the boulder erected to the memory of Sagamore John.

Originally published in vol. 33, 1930.

Opposite: Monument to Sagamore John, chief of the Mystic tribe. The monument was erected on the Brooks Estate by Francis Brooks in 1884.

HOW DID MEDFORD GET ITS NAME?

The first mention of Medford is in the colony record of the General Court, under date of September 28, 1630, when three pounds were levied upon it for the support of military instructors.

Under the same date a coroner's jury returned its verdict in the death of Austin Bratcher at Mr. Cradock's farm, which resulted in the indictment of Walter Palmer for manslaughter and his subsequent acquittal from the charge in November. But one of Cradock's "servants" held variant opinion and sought "to traduce the court," and was sentenced to be whipped therefore, being the fifth in the colony to receive such a sentence.

Here we find Medford's entrance into the limelight of history. Mr. Cradock's farm was a tract of land a mile wide (approximately) and four miles along the riverside from Charlestown, which then extended some fifteen miles northwestward.

The Indians who lived there were called Aberginians, and their name comes down to us today, in that of the Aberjona, the upper reach of their river, the tidal stream they called Missi-tuk, which the English tongue called Mistick.

The misty Mystic River at Rock Hill.

That it was the locality is proven by Josselyn in 1638, as "three miles from Charlestown and a league and a half, four and one-half miles, by water, i.e., by the winding or circuitous river's course." He applied the name Mistick to the little settlement on the northwest side of the river. So here are three names of one and the same place, all contemporary: first, Medford, from the colony record; second, Mr. Cradock's farm, also from the colony record; third, Mistick, from Josselyn, is of Indian origin. The second was proprietary, but would of necessity be in time outgrown and disused. The third was official and remains. But why Medford? Towns are named by governmental, executive or legislative action, in honor or memory of persons or places, as well as peculiarities. But we search the colony records in vain to find that Mr. Cradock's farm is called Medford; and literally speaking, the early Medford was never incorporated. Like Topsy, she simply "growed." Still the fact remains that in September 1630, a tax of three pounds had been laid upon a place designated by the General Court as Medford and again we ask, "Why Medford?" When and by whom previously? There are no local records to search—really none until 1674. We can only answer the query by the result of reason and research. We have already noted the geographical situation of Mr. Cradock's farm, the early Medford.

The seventeenth of June 1630 is commonly accepted, and 275 years after was celebrated, as the time of settlement, and again we may ask why. Because Governor Winthrop wrote, "We went up Mistick river about six miles." Winthrop did not settle in Medford but in Charlestown, on the other side of the river. However, as seen in Deputy Governor Dudley's letter (of March 28, 1631) to the Countess of Lincoln, of those coming from Salem, some "found a good place upon Mistick…which we named Meadford." Here then is the earliest authentic account we have of the naming of Medford. Again in our search we ask, "Why Medford?" and answer our own query, thus— Because the "good place upon Mistick" was to be Mr. Cradock's farm, and they so called it from Medford in Staffordshire in the old England they came from, and which old shire Mr. Cradock had represented in Parliament since 1620, the eighteenth year of the reign of James the first.

As we had no dictograph record of Dudley's pronunciation, we have naturally considered that M-e-a-d was pronounced phonetically as Meed, and so has come the usual interpretation of Medford, as Meadow-ford, though in 1855, historian Brooks gave it as "great-meadow," making no mention therewith of the fording place he knew to have existed. He directly tells us that in one of the earliest deeds of sale it is written "Metford," and that after 1715 it has been uniformly written "Medford." Meadowford would not have been an inappropriate designation for a specific place in the river's course; but ancient Medford or Mr. Cradock's farm was four miles long.

Governor Winthrop meets Mayor Larkin and colonial ladies at the tercentenary celebration in 1930. *From left to right*: Mrs. J.D. Robinson, Mrs. Hollis E. Gray, Mayor Larkin, Edwin F. Pidgeon as Winthrop, Mrs. Elizabeth L. McGray and Mrs. Forrest O. Batchelder.

Glimpses of Medford: Selections from the Historical Register

Now a few words relative to Metford, and copy of a written note attached to a copy of *History of Medford* (Brooks) by Caleb Swan, which is of interest, and never before published.

Medford, July 31, 1857.

Mr. Charles Brooks (the author of this book) dining with us at Dr. Swan's today—Mrs Adams and daughter of Winter hill being present—said that he had lately ascertained that the original name of the town was Metford—after a county seat Governor Cradock in England in Staffordshire called Metford and that he named his new town from that and that in his will he called it Metford in New England.

In Surveys of Staffordshire Preface p. XVI is mention by a contemporary diarist, of R. Caverswall house Mr Cradock owns it.

And elsewhere in same book is 1640, 15 Ch.[arles] *I Matthew Cradock Eng. merchant returned to Parliament for the City of London. The last Matthew Cradock built the house at Caverswall.*

To our caption query we reply: The original settlement of Medford was by men in the employ and interest of Matthew Cradock, merchant of London. He was the first governor or president of a trading company chartered by King Charles I. He never came oversea but suggested the transfer here of the charter that became the foundation of a commonwealth.

Old home associations such as Mr. Brooks alluded to at Dr. Swan's dinner table (also alluded to by the English diarist quoted) may have prompted him to call the new plantation he was starting Medford or Metford. Dudley, his associate and successor in office, writes, "which we named Meadford," thus differing slightly in possible pronunciation.

Whether "d" or "t" is of little moment, but it is tantalizing that Mr. Brooks failed to mention the sources of his information regarding the Staffordshire town. Called in *Domesday Book* both Medford and Metford, in 1173 it was called Medford. In 1251 it was still Medford, later it was Mefford; and in 1892, and probably now, Meaford—all this variety of spelling (possibly not of pronunciation) in staid old England. Somehow we fancy that "e" has its short sound in all, as a recent comer from Staffordshire pronounces the present Meaford "Mefford." The New England town, now a city of 37,000 people, has almost from its earliest days been called Medford and sixteen others in as many states bear the name spelled in the same way and more or less traceable thereto.

We have tried to answer the query on lines of historic truth, citing only credible evidence. Our readers must decide for themselves, much as did the children who asked which was the lion and which the baboon, and were told by the accommodating showman, "Just which you pleases, little dears, you pays your money and you takes your choice." Our choice is: Medford got its name from Medford in Staffordshire, Old England.

Originally published in vol. 22, 1919.

THE LEGEND OF "CHEESE ROCK"

The famous "Cheese Rock" on Bear Hill in the Middlesex Fells where Governor Winthrop ate his lunch.

[For the Forest Festival, June 7, 1882]

In sixteen hundred thirty-one
   It was a winter day,
When Winthrop, Nowell, Eliot,
   To northward strolled away.

The frozen Mistick flood they crossed,
   Ere Cradock's mansion stood;

O'er swamps and rocky hills they pressed,
  Through miles of lofty wood.

They crossed a lovely ice-bound lake,
  With islands here and there;
"Spot Pond" they called it, from the rocks
  That showed their noddles bare.

Then up northwestwardly they climbed,
  A hill well crowned with trees,
And hungry there, as well might be,
  They dined on simple cheese.

For, why? the guv'nor's man in haste,
  And careless how they fed,
His basket loaded with the cheese
  And quite forgot the bread.

This fact so simple and so grand,
  To us they handed down;
"Cheese Rock" they named that lovely hill,
  Those men of high renown.

Some smaller men cut off the trees
  And then they named it "Bare";
And when the bushes wildly grew
  They spelled it "B-e-a-r."

But nature still asserts her rights
  Against all vulgar spells,
And cries aloud, "Restore the pines
  To these my favorite Fells.

Mount Winthrop you may call this spot
  If you'll preserve the trees
That canopied with winter's green
  The guv'nor's lunch of cheese!"

Originally published in vol. 14, 1911.

MEDFORD SQUARE IN THE EARLY DAYS
Moses Whitcher Mann

My instructions read thus—"You are to tell of Medford Square as it has been." So I will begin with its earliest known time.

Three hundred years ago it was only the home and haunt of Native Americans. Across it lay the trail or beaten path they made in their journeyings and on which our three streets, Main, Salem and High, converge. Near that junction was a small pond and a little way upstream the river was fordable. Opposite that ford the hill rose abruptly high with only a narrow passage at its foot along the river's edge.

A former Medford man in writing of his native town said, referring to the eastern and western parts, "Medford was a spectacle town, a bulky red nose stuck up between the glasses." The surface of that nose was dark red gravel, but the bones behind it are the darker Medford granite that shows now so plainly up Governors Avenue.

A ship on the Mystic River, circa 1900, looking west toward Cradock Bridge.

GLIMPSES OF MEDFORD: SELECTIONS FROM THE HISTORICAL REGISTER

The earliest white men to come here were Captain Myles Standish and eight others from the Pilgrim settlement at Plymouth on September 21, 1621, and it was said they liked it here so well that they wished they had been settled here. In 1629 came an exploring party overland from Salem, then but just settled, and found established here a company of men who were in the employ of one Matthew Cradock, a wealthy London merchant.

They had erected some log houses for shelter, and were building a small vessel for their fishing. Their work was a business adventure of Cradock's, of which he had several, besides the corporate affairs of the Massachusetts Bay Colony, of which he was the president, or governor, as they styled him. And because they did so, do we call our chief magistrate governor. This exploring party found the Mystic valley and ponds "a country full of stately timber and some Indians called Aberginians," whether because they were aborigines (dwellers from beginning) or not, we may not say.

Several early travelers mention this settlement as "a scattered village with but few houses as yet" and tell of a "park impaled in which cattle were kept till Cradock could stock it with deer."

Such facts are the meager information we have of the earliest Medford. Remember that the country here was then a wilderness, its animal life wild, the former human life barbarous, even savage. And remember, also, that it was not Pilgrim Plymouth or Puritan Boston that sent those first settlers here to occupy this territory and prepare the way for those later residents who became that body politic we call a town.

They occupied a tract of land four miles along this side of the river and about a mile wide. They were called Cradock's servants, workmen of various trades, and in 1634 the tract was granted to their employer as his farm or plantation. They gave it the manorial name of Mead-ford or Medford (from his English country seat) and the principal building became known as Meadford House.

Its owner never came over from England and so never saw his New England possession. It and his business affairs were managed by his agents, Mayhew, Davison and lastly Edward Collins, who, some years after Cradock's death, purchased the whole farm of the heirs.

Now, as I have told thus of those long-ago times and place, have you formed a mental picture of how this neighboring territory we call Medford Square looked then, and of the few people here located along the banks of the Mystic River?

In those days the place was also called M-i-s-t-i-c-k, from the Indian name of the river Missi-tuk, which meant great tidal river. But there was nothing mystical or mysterious about it. It was the Englishman's way of pronouncing the Indian word—and by and by he spelled it M-y-s-t-i-c-k-e, and later, abbreviated into our common Mystic. I trust you have also seen that those early comers of Cradock's venture antedated the Puritan settlers of Charlestown and Boston by one—perhaps two—years. I know our town seal said Medford—Condita—1630, but Cradock's men came in 1629 or 1628. But with the coming of Governor Winthrop with King Charles's charter, their squatter sovereignty ceased and all were under the authority of the Great and General Court.

I really wish the first mention of Medford in the authentic records of that court was of a pleasanter nature to quote, but I remember that the late James Hervey said, "If we are to be historical we must tell the truth." Under date of September 23, 1630, we read that "one Austin Bratcher, dying lately at Mr. Cradock's plantation, a jury found that the strokes given by Walter Palmer were accounted manslaughter." But two months later, Palmer (who was from Charlestown) was acquitted, not to the satisfaction of everybody, as one Thomas Fox was fined for saying the court had been bribed. An unpleasant episode—Medford's entrance into the limelight of history.

During the first ten years the fording place was used in crossing the river, unless a boat or raft served, but in 1639 the agent Davison had a bridge built a little way below. It was 150 feet long, very narrow and but little above the marshes that bordered the river. And very soon he found his good work had got him into trouble, as his employer's farm was only on this side, and this structure, desirable as it was, was half in the adjoining town of Charlestown. So troubles of various kinds came up, and towns west and north were called upon to assist in its maintenance for nearly a century. Davison must have gotten roiled up some over it for he was brought up before the court for swearing an oath, and fined.

In 1640 Captain Edward Johnson and others came up from Charlestown over this new way and bridge and turned about by the little pond and along the varge way, following the old trail across the brook and up another hill and then northwesterly about five miles, and settled Waterfield and Charlestown Village. Two years later they organized a church, and were incorporated by the General Court in this terse, brief form: "Charlestown Village is called Wooburne."

With this and other going to and fro, our country roads may be said to have begun. The Salem path easterly, of course, was older. An interesting incident is told in Governor Winthrop's diary about one of the earliest mentioned women in Medford. The story reads:

> One Dalkin of Medford, with his wife, had been to Cambridge for the Sabbath, and returning found the tide too high at the ford for a safe passage. Dalkin got over but told his better-half to wait for the tide to recede; but she

*persisted in crossing, and losing her footing was borne along by the current.
Dalkin shouted loudly for help and their faithful dog plunged in after his
mistress, who, seizing the dog's tail, was safely towed ashore.*

Another road was in time developed, first called "the way to Blanchard's."
Blanchard was the owner of a house built in 1657, then in Malden, but now
by annexation in Medford, the oldest house in our city. We know it as the
Blanchard-Bradbury-Wellington House. Next, this road was Distil-house
lane, later Ship Street and now Riverside Avenue.

Unlike every other place in the colony, there was no house of worship
here until 1696, and no church formed until 1712. Neither was Medford
represented in the General Court until 1689, sixty years after its settlement.
Its growth had been very slow. The purchasers of its 2,450 acres were but
four. In two generations their numbers were still small, increased by a few
newcomers like Peter Tufts and the Wades and Brookses. Two of their
substantial houses remain today. When they built the first public building
(note they called it their meetinghouse), they found their central location,
not here by the road-junction and bridge, but a half-mile westward, on a
great rock beside "Oborn Rode." And so in their anomalous position, with
no local government, they applied to the General Court to be orientated.
And they found out, by getting this brief answer, "Medford hath been and
is a peculiar and hath privileges as other towns as to prudentials."

This enactment was a little more verbose than "Charlestown Village is called Wooburne" or "Sagust is called Linn," and is the nearest approach to incorporation Medford ever had as a town. But mind this: it was not Medford is a peculiar town, as Mr. Brooks in his history says, but "a peculiar." Our genial city clerk can show you that word peculiar used as a noun in the old record book, which I have myself read, and it is an exact copy of the colony or province record in the Massachusetts archives. Having thus been shown the way, the Medford people got busy about their "prudentials as other towns" and organized a local town government.

Originally published in vol. 28, 1925.

Opposite: The Blanchard-Wellington-Bradbury House on Bradbury Avenue. Built before 1650.

Chapter 2

REVOLUTIONARY TIMES

MEDFORD AND THE TEA TAX
Elizabeth Estes

When the rest of the Townshend Acts were repealed in 1770, the tax on tea was kept to help establish the authority of Parliament. Every town resented the tax and took action against it. In November 1774, a warrant was issued to the voters of Medford to meet and decide what action, if any, should be taken in regard to the selling and drinking of East India tea. At this meeting they "voted that we will not use any East India Teas in our Families till the Acts be Repealed" and also appointed a committee consisting of Benjamin Hall, Deacon Kidder, Deacon Warren, Caleb Brooks and others to post in some public place the names of those found selling or using tea in their families.

Later we find that the town, being informed that "severall ships were already arrived in Boston with large quantities [of tea] on board and severall more daily expected," therefore, "to Prevent the many formidable evils consequent upon the Success of this alarming & subtle attempts to rivet the Chains of oppression," they

> *Resolved 1ˢᵗ. That it is the incumbent duty of all free British Subjects in America to Unite in the use of all lawfull measures necessary and expedient for the preservation and security of their rights and priviledges, civil and Religious.*

2nd. That it is the opinion of this Town, that the British parliment have no constitutional authority to tax these colonies without their own consent and that therefore the present duty laid upon teas imported here from Great Briton for the purpose of a Revenue, is a tax illegally laid upon and extorted from us.

3rd. That sd. India Company, exporting their own teas to the Colonies while charged with sd. duty, has a direct tendency to establish sd. Revenue act.

4th. That we will exert ourselves and join with our American bretheren in adopting and prosecuting all Legall and proper measures to discourage and prevent ye landing storing and vending and using those Teas among us, and that whosoever shall aid or assist sd. India Company, their Factors or Servants in either Landing, Storing or Selling the same does a manifest injury to his Country and deserves to be treated with severity and contempt.

5th. That we are ready at all times in conjunction with our American bretheren as Loyall subjects to risque our lives and Fortunes in the service and defence of his Majesty's person, crown & dignity and also as a free people in asserting and maintaining, inviolate our civil and Religious rights and priviledges against all opposers whatever.

6th. That the thanks of this Town be and are hereby given to our worthy bretheren in the Town of Boston for their unwearied care and pains in endeavoring to preserve our rights and priviledges free from innovation and furnishing this and our other Towns with Copies of their late proceedings.

The stubbornness of the king, however, was proof against all such petitions, and a Revolutionary War compelled what a narrow statesmanship had refused to grant.

Originally published in vol. 3, 1900.

MEDFORD AND HER MINUTEMEN, APRIL 19, 1775
Richard B. Coolidge

In Medford, as in the neighboring cities and towns, we meet today in memory of the men and the events of April 19, 1775. On that day and in this region roundabout began the American Revolution. For that reason the nineteenth of April, in whatever year it falls, speaks for itself. Today, after the passing of a century and a half, it speaks significantly to us, citizens of the great and prosperous America, whose beginnings were in the first armed stand of the Minutemen gathered from the towns roundabout us.

In the late evening of April 18 the waning moon cast a fantasy of light and shadow over the sleeping town. Down from the hills to the north, almost to the river bottom, spread the dark forest, the Charlestown wood lots of earlier years, with Pine Hill rising in their midst. Along the Mystic ran the way to the weirs. From the crossroads near Cradock's bridge ran the road to Charlestown, and from the same point, later the marketplace, led the road to Salem. Along these highways were gathered most of the houses, but little over a hundred in number, where dwelt less than a thousand townspeople. Up the road to Menotomy the moonlight fell upon the steeple of the third meetinghouse, silent in its mid-week desertion. Beyond the square, about an equal distance down the road to Charlestown, it greeted the last flickering candlelight in the Admiral Vernon. There, too, the vague rumors of the day, discussed at the tavern bar over many a round of "flip," were lulled in the quiet of the surrounding night. Medford slept.

A dramatic Paul Revere reenacts the historic visit to the Isaac Hall House on High Street Patriot's Day, circa 1905.

In the last hour of that restless day two spots of light carried their rays from the steeple of the North Church in Boston up the valley of the Mystic. With the new day, the nineteenth, a horse and rider burst over the crest of Winter Hill and dashed down the slope along the road from Charlestown into the sleeping town. On the left, as he drew nearer the bridge, the rider passed the mansion house of Isaac Royall, set back in the midst of its ample estate. The glint of moonlight fell upon its darkened windows, for Colonel Royall, the Sunday previous, had ridden off in his chariot to Boston, and was then and thereafter absent from Medford.

Across the Mystic, at the town square, the horse and rider turned to the left into the road to Menotomy. There on the right stood the house of Isaac Hall, captain of the Minutemen. Here he drew rein. A knock on the door, a hurried alarm and with the prompt response of candlelight from within, Medford was again astir. Up the road to Menotomy the messenger of the night pressed on, by the dark meetinghouse on the right, up the slope of Marm Simond's hill, by the house of Jonathan Brooks, still standing at the fork of the Woburn road, over the bridge at the weirs, into Menotomy and on toward Lexington. So Paul Revere came into Medford, and so, lost in the moonlight and the shadows of the lonely road, he left it.

It was at Captain Hall's house that he made his first stop on that night ride. But, in his own language, after leaving Captain Hall's, he gave the alarm at almost every house on the way to Lexington.

It is not recorded at what hour of the night Captain Hall assembled his company of Minutemen. It is certain that from midnight to sunrise, in house after house, the flicker of candlelight revealed the household aroused, the flintlock and powder horn passed by hands trembling with excitement to the father or brother who, swinging on his accoutrements, hurried out into the night. Doubtless before sunrise every household knew that the British Regulars were moving toward Concord and that the moment of action had come.

Of the fifty-nine Minutemen who trooped up the road to Menotomy where Paul Revere had passed at midnight, nine bore the name of Tufts and five the name of Hall. We leave them, then, for a moment tramping along the road beyond the bridge at the weirs, alert, determined, grasping their flintlocks in the firm grip of men certain of danger but uncertain at what corner of the road it may face them.

The townspeople left behind did not idly leave the business of the day to the fifty-nine who had marched off. After daybreak the town was almost destitute of men, for unorganized volunteers, singly and in groups, took up their own hurried march, eager to be in the fray. One was Henry Putnam, in 1758 a lieutenant in the Louisburg campaign, and past the age of military service. Seizing his flintlock as his wife asked if he were going without his dinner, he answered, "I am going to take powder and balls for my dinner today, or to give them some." Another participant was the Reverend Edward Brooks. From his house near the old slave wall on the Grove Street of today, he too went over to Lexington, and with full-bottomed wig rode on horseback, his gun on his shoulder.

As the day wore on armed provincials from other towns trooped through the town. The road between Medford and Salem was the highway leading to the country northeast of Boston. To Malden a horseman from Medford dashed along this road in the early morning, scattering the alarm. His name is lost. The clanging of the meetinghouse bell, then on Bell Rock, brought the townspeople of Malden to the Kettell's tavern. There seventy-six men under Captain Benjamin Blaney assembled, and with drums beating, marched to Medford under orders to proceed to Watertown. Near Cradock Bridge the company halted while the whereabouts of the British was verified, and then at noon proceeded through the town to Menotomy.

But what, meantime, was the business of Captain Hall and his company who marched off under the waning moon, pressing on after Paul Revere?

Medford's Minutemen march again on Patriot's Day, circa 1905.

GLIMPSES OF MEDFORD: SELECTIONS FROM THE HISTORICAL REGISTER

It was about half-past ten in the evening of April eighteenth that eight hundred British Regulars under Lieutenant Colonel Smith, having assembled at the foot of Boston Common, now Boylston Street, embarked across the Charles for Lechmere point in East Cambridge. There began their midnight march to Lexington through Cambridge, both to capture Hancock and Adams and to destroy the provincial stores. The expedition was intended to be secret. To prevent his movements from becoming known, General Gage sent out ten or more sergeants, posted along the highways in Cambridge and toward Concord. It was while the troops at rest on the Cambridge shore were receiving a day's rations and thirty-six rounds of ammunition that Revere started from the Charlestown shore, mounted on Deacon Larkin's best horse. He had gone beyond Charlestown Neck, along the Cambridge Road to the point where Crescent Street now joins Washington Street in Somerville, when he caught sight of two British officers halted in the shadows by the roadside. Wheeling his horse, he dashed back along the road to the Neck and turned into the Mystic Road, now Broadway and Main Street in Somerville, and Main Street in Medford. It was the two British officers who intercepted Revere on his intended route to Cambridge that caused him to make the detour through Medford. It is because of those unknown soldiers of the night, lurking in the shadows of the road, that in Medford and at the house of Isaac Hall the first alarm was sounded on that ride.

It was one o'clock before the British column left the Charles River behind them. By that time Revere was in Lexington, and one hour earlier than that Medford had the news that the British were moving. By two o'clock the king's men were in the present Union Square, Somerville. By three o'clock, coming up the Lexington and Concord road, now Massachusetts Avenue, they had halted at the present Arlington Center. Indeed, the Sons of Liberty were aware of the intended march even before the troops themselves. In more than one house along the route, as the steady tramp of the advancing column awakened the householders, they peered out upon the strange sight of the passing redcoats. Signal guns and alarm bells rapidly spread the news, and here in Arlington, Smith, realizing the significance of the signal guns and alarm bells, sent back to General Gage for reinforcements.

At five o'clock the troops had covered the eleven miles to Lexington. There on the Common, just before sunrise, the light infantry, under Major Pitcairn, exchanged the first volleys with Captain Parker's Minutemen who stood in the path of the invading army.

Here, as the Minutemen fell at sunrise, war began. To the British that encounter was little more than a skirmish. In half an hour, with fife and drum and flying colors, the column moved up the road. By eight o'clock Smith's main body had reached its objective six miles farther on in Concord.

There they searched out the stores, and there, between the hours of nine and ten, their advance turned into a retreat in the battle of the North Bridge.

It is not easy to determine the whereabouts of the Minutemen from Medford during the entire advance of the British toward Concord. The hour of their starting is not recorded, although one historian writes that they were early on the march. Nor is the precise extent of their march known. During the British advance to Lexington the troops were unmolested by armed provincials. At Lexington, Captain Parker's men alone barred the way.

Major General John Brooks, later governor of Massachusetts.

Out of Concord about a mile is Merriam's Corner, and here it is commonly said that Captain Hall's men fell in with the Reading company under Major John Brooks. Here the battle suspended at the North Bridge was renewed, with fatalities on both sides. At this point American reinforcements came in, to the number of 1,147, bringing their forces, at the most, up to 1,500, somewhat less than the 5,000 who appeared in the exaggerated vision of the ensign. In no formal list of the reinforcements do the Medford men appear. Tradition, however, is to the contrary.

For present purposes we may again adopt the words of De Bernice when, in reference to the progress of the troops through Lincoln into Lexington, he wrote, "The Provincials kept the road always lined and a very hot fire on us without intermission. We began to run rather than retreat in order." So, too, later reported his lieutenant colonel that the firing on his troops "increased to a very great degree and continued without the intermission of five minutes altogether for, I believe, upwards of eighteen miles."

If the Medford men were not among the provincials who carried on the running attack both on the main column and the flanking parties, there was other business for them along the road below Lexington.

When Smith reached Arlington on his advance twelve hours earlier, alarmed by the general uprising that was becoming evident, he sent back to General Gage for reinforcements. One thousand men under Lord Percy proceeded to his relief. Their progress from Boston Neck through Roxbury, Brighton, Cambridge and Arlington was not unmolested. At Arlington, for instance, the old men of Menotomy lay in wait and captured his entire baggage train, driving the horses off to Medford. Between two and three o'clock his column reached Lexington about opposite the present high school and there, opening their ranks, received into that welcome shelter Smith's exhausted troops.

It was nearly four o'clock when the British forces again moved. Their progress, marked by pillage and burning, evidenced Percy's conception of the warfare that his exigencies warranted. The Minutemen, now bitterly aroused, continued the attack down the road into the present Arlington. There the Americans, under General Heath and Doctor Warren, rallied and attacked Percy's rear guard. Here some 1,800 men reinforced the provincials. Among these companies are all those who are definitely known to have marched through Medford to Menotomy earlier in the day. Here are listed as entering the battle Captain Hall of Medford, 59 men; Captain Blaney of Malden, 75 men; Captain Bancroft of Lynn, 38 men; and eight companies of Danvers men, totaling 331 men. It thus appears that these companies, among others, may have been definitely held at Menotomy, or in the uncertainty that attended the direction of the unorganized American forces, that they awaited the developments of the day at this point. At the base of Pierce's Hill, now Arlington Heights, the battle raged along the highway to Arlington Center. Between the house of Jason Russell, still standing on Jason Street, and the center of the village, the fighting reached its climax. Altogether in Arlington on that afternoon 25 provincials fell or were mortally wounded. Among them were Henry Putnam and William Polly of Medford.

It was between five and six o'clock that Percy crossed into Cambridge, then into the present city of Somerville at the corner of Beach and Elm Streets, down Somerville Avenue into Union Square and so on down Washington Street along the then–Cambridge Road. Soon after sunset the column reached Charlestown Common, now Sullivan Square, and wheeled up Bunker Hill. The British were back in Charlestown.

All along this route the Minutemen kept up the attack upon the exhausted and disordered British, sometimes in organized attack, sometimes in personal encounter. Among the troops that followed the British down into Charlestown were the Minutemen of Medford.

Memorial to Medford's Revolutionary War soldiers, located in front of the library on the corner of Hillside and High Streets.

So ended the battle of April 19, and while the women and children of Charlestown were fleeing in terror across the marshes to Medford, the Medford company proceeded to Cambridge, which became the headquarters of the American army.

But how looked at these events Hugh Earl Percy, whose men that night recrossed the Charles in the boats of the *Somerset*, which swung in the tide as Paul Revere, the night before, passed under its shadow?

To the Duke of Northumberland he wrote on August 18, 1775, "My dearest Father...I have enclosed a newspaper containing copies of some letters wrote by some of the principal people at the Congress, who were intercepted by us. You will perceive from them that their aim is (what I am convinced it has ever been) Independence."

Originally published in vol. 28, 1925.

Captain Isaac Hall
Hall Gleason

Isaac Hall, son of Andrew and Abigail (Walker) Hall, was born in Medford January 24, 1739, in the house now standing at the corner of High Street and Bradlee Road.

His father died when he was eleven years of age, and he continued to live there with his mother, who took the estate as part of her dower. The estate is described as bounded southerly by the country road, westerly on Henry Fowle's land and easterly on land of Thomas Seacomb and Joseph Thompson.

Isaac was employed by his brother, Benjamin Hall, a distiller, until January 27, 1775, when he was taken into partnership, and we find a record of the purchase of a distillery from Jno. Dexter by the firm.

October 8, 1761, Isaac was married to Abigail, daughter of Ebenezer and Sarah Cutter of Medford, and he and his bride lived with his widowed mother until her death in 1785, in the dower house, and here eight children were born to them.

Isaac was the captain of the Medford Minutemen, and when the storm of war that had been gathering broke at last, the men of Medford were among the first to respond and perform their share in the War for Independence. Paul Revere in his personal narrative tells how he had crossed the river, passing the British man-of-war *Somerset*; had mounted Deacon Larkin's horse and started on his ride, intending to pass over Charlestown Neck and over through Cambridge. Near what is now Sullivan Square he met two British officers who tried to stop him. He turned and pushed for the Medford road, and got clear of them. He says, "I went through Medford over the bridge and up to Menotomy. In Medford I waked the Captain of the Minute Men, and after that, I alarmed almost every house till I got to Lexington."

Miss Helen T. Wild in her *History of Medford in the Revolution* says, "Captn Hall and his company marched to Lexington and there joined Captn John Brooks and his Reading company…The combined companies met the British at Merriam's Corner and followed them to Charlestown Ferry, continuing their fire until the last of the troops had embarked." The Medford company was in the Thirty-seventh Massachusetts Regiment, commanded by Colonel Thomas Gardner. In the account of the Battle of Bunker Hill in his *Siege of Boston*, Frothingham says,

> *After the British landed, this regiment* [Gardner's] *was stationed in the road leading to Lechmere's Point, and late in the day was ordered to Charlestown. On arriving at Bunker Hill, General Putnam ordered part of it to assist in throwing up defences commenced at this place. One company* [Harris's] *went to the rail fence. The greater part under the lead of their colonel on the third attack advanced towards the redoubt. On the way, Colonel Gardner was struck by a ball, which inflicted a mortal wound.*

The loss of the regiment in this battle was six killed, seven wounded.

September 1, 1775, Isaac Hall was discharged to organize another company of men from Medford, Stoneham and other adjoining towns. With this company he marched to Dorchester Heights in March 1776. During 1775 and 1776 he acted as commissary for the troops that were quartered here. His business affairs had evidently suffered from his absence on military duties. He and his brothers also lost large sums from furnishing the government with rum and other medical and military supplies, and receiving payment in a constantly depreciating currency. In 1778 he was assessed for a tax of about thirty pounds in gold. In 1789, the year of his death, his tax had decreased to four pounds in currency. In 1787 he sold his distillery to his brother, Ebenezer, and all that was not conveyed to him he sold to J.C. Jones. In August 1789, he disposed of the remainder of his property to Ebenezer.

He took an active part in town affairs and served as a town officer in different capacities from 1765 to 1789, the year of his death. He held, at different times, the office of engine-man, wood corder, salt-measurer, assessor and fire warden. At a town meeting held in May 1789, it was "voted to petition the General Court for a lottery, to widen the bridge and pave the market place, so called." Isaac Hall was appointed a member of the committee.

The Captain Isaac Hall House on High Street in Medford Square.

Dedication of the Captain Isaac Hall memorial by the Sons of the Revolution, June 14, 1905.

Among his friends was Colonel Isaac Royall, who "halted between two opinions respecting the revolution, until the cannonading at Lexington drove him to Newburyport and then to Halifax." In Brooks's *History of Medford* is an account of an examination respecting the political behavior of Colonel Royall. Among the persons examined was Captain Isaac Hall, who declared: "That the winter before said battle [Lexington] he went to settle accounts with said Royall at his house; and that said Royall showed him his arms and accoutrements (which were in very good order), and told him that he determined to stand for his country."

Isaac Hall died November 24, 1789. A sword, said to be the one he carried at Lexington and Bunker Hill, is in the possession of James L. Hall of Kingston, Massachusetts. It was left him by Mrs. Susan M. Fitch, who received it from her grandfather, Ebenezer Hall, a brother of Isaac.

The tablet is not intended to perpetuate any remarkable military achievements of valor of Captain Isaac Hall, though he performed his part in those heroic contests that gave confidence to the colonists in their resistance to oppression. It is more that Medford desires to honor all the men who helped her to take so important a share in the early battles of the war that gave birth to the nation, and which has meant freedom for the whole English-speaking race.

Originally published in vol. 8, 1905.

SARAH BRADLEE FULTON
Helen Tilden Wild

The names of the men who fought in the War of the American Revolution are carefully preserved in the archives of the state, but the women who through all those sad years endured hardship and loss, and who toiled at the spinning wheel and in the hospitals for their country's cause, have long ago been forgotten. Only here and there a woman's name is found on the honor roll of Revolutionary days.

Among the Medford women whom history has remembered, Sarah Bradlee Fulton has a prominent place. We have been proud to name our chapter for her, honoring with her all the unknown loyal women who worked and prayed in this dear old town of ours for the cause of liberty.

Mrs. Fulton was a member of the Bradlee family of Dorchester and Boston. In 1762 she married John Fulton, and ten years later they came to

Medford with their little sons and daughters and made their home on the east side of Main Street about 150 feet south of the bridge, on the south side of what is now Tufts Place. Her brother, Nathaniel Bradlee, lived in Boston at the corner of Tremont and Hollis Streets. The old house is still standing and occupied by his descendants.

His carpenter's shop, and his kitchen on Saturday nights when friends and neighbors gathered to enjoy his codfish suppers, were meeting places for Boston's most devoted Patriots. From this shop a detachment of Mohawks who "turned Boston Harbor into a teapot" went forth to their work of destruction. In the kitchen Mrs. Bradlee and Mrs. Fulton disguised the master of the house and several of his comrades, and later heated water in the great copper boiler and provided all that was needed to transform these Indians into respectable Bostonians. Nathaniel Bradlee's principles were well known, and a spy, hoping to find some proof against him, peered in at the kitchen window, but saw these two women moving about so quietly and naturally that he passed on, little dreaming what was really in progress there.

A year and a half later Sarah Fulton heard the alarm of Paul Revere as "he crossed the bridge into Medford town," and a few days after the place became the headquarters of General Stark's New Hampshire regiment.

Then came the battle of Bunker Hill. All day the people of Medford watched the battle with anxious hearts; many a son and brother were there—dying, maybe, just out of their reach. At sunset the wounded were brought into town, and the large open space by Wade's Tavern between the bridge and South Street was turned into a field hospital. Surgeons were few, but the women did their best as nurses. Among them, the steady nerves of Sarah Fulton made her a leader. One poor fellow had a bullet in his cheek, and she removed it; she almost forgot the circumstance until, years after, he came to thank her for her service.

During the siege of Boston, detachments of British soldiers often came across the river under protection of their ships, searching for fuel in Medford. One day a load of wood intended for the troops at Cambridge was expected to come through town, and one of these bands of soldiers was there before it. Sarah Fulton, knowing that the wood would be lost unless something was done, and hoping that private property would be respected, sent her husband to meet the team, buy the load and bring it home. He carried out the first part of the program, but on the way to the house he met the soldiers, who seized the wood.

When his wife heard the story she flung on a shawl and went in pursuit. Overtaking the party, she took the oxen by the horns and turned them round. The men threatened to shoot her, but she shouted defiantly as she started her team, "Shoot away!" Astonishment, admiration and amusement were too much for the Regulars, and they unconditionally surrendered.

Sarah Bradlee Fulton's heirs, the Ladies of the Revolutionary Group, at the tercentenary celebration in 1930. The Medford chapter of the DAR bears Fulton's name.

...ion 1930

...d, June 23, 24, 25 + 30.   July 1 + 2, 1930

...roup

Soon after, Major Brooks, later our honored governor, was given dispatches by General Washington that must be delivered inside the enemy's lines. Late one night he came to John Fulton, knowing his patriotism and his intimate knowledge of Boston, and asked him to undertake the trust. He was not able to go, but his wife volunteered. Her offer was accepted.

A long, lonely and dangerous walk it was to the waterside in Charlestown, but she reached there in safety and, finding a boat, rowed across the river. Cautiously making her way to the place she sought, she delivered her dispatches and returned as she had come. When the first streak of dawn appeared, she stood safe on her own door-stone.

In recognition of her services General Washington visited her. It is said that according to the fashion of the day John Fulton, on this occasion, brewed a potation whose chief ingredient was the far-famed product of the town. The little silver-mounted ladle was dipped in the steaming concoction, and the first glass from Mrs. Fulton's new punch bowl was sipped by His Excellency. This was the proudest day of Sarah Fulton's life. The chair in which he sat and the punch bowl and ladle were always sacred, and are still treasured by her descendants.

Years later, General Lafayette was her guest, and we can safely say he was seated in General Washington's chair, served with punch from that same punch bowl and entertained with the story of that memorable visit.

Sarah Fulton was never afraid of man or beast; as she once told her little grandson, she "never turned her back on anything." Her strength of mind was matched by her strength of body. After the Revolution she made her home on the old road to Stoneham, which at the first town meeting after her death was named Fulton Street in her honor. More than a mile from the square, the cellar of the house can still be seen, and many Medford people remember the building itself.

In spite of the long distance Sarah Fulton, even in extreme old age, was in the habit of walking to and from the Unitarian church every Sunday. Those who knew her could scarcely comprehend that she had passed four-score years and ten.

She saw grandchildren and great-grandchildren grow up around her, and in the atmosphere of their love and reverence she spent her last days.

One night in November 1835, a month before her ninety-fifth birthday, she lay down to sleep, and in the morning her daughters found her lying with a peaceful smile on her face—dead. They laid her in the old Salem Street cemetery, and there she sleeps among her old friends and neighbors.

Originally published in vol. 1, 1898.

Chapter 3

SHIPBUILDING

EARLIEST MYSTIC RIVER SHIPBUILDING
John H. Hooper

October 15-1635. A number of Dorchester, Mass., families began their journey to Windsor, Conn., and arrived at their destination just as winter was setting in. Many died of cold and starvation. In December about 70 adults and children, including some of these emigrants came to Saybrook from the up-river settlement and took passage for Boston in the *Rebecca*, a vessel of 60 tons burden."

"April 26-1636. The possessions of William Pynchon and others, who settled Springfield, Mass., were sent to the head of navigation on the Connecticut, in the *Blessing of the Bay* belonging to Gov. John Winthrop."

The *Rebecca* was owned by Governor Mathew Cradock, and was, no doubt, built in Medford soon after the settlement of the plantation.

The establishment of his men on the Mystic, extensively employed in the fisheries, caused the building of small vessels therefore, and this leads to the inference that shipbuilding was commenced on the Mystic at an early date.

In a letter from the company in London to the authorities here, dated April 17, 1629, they say, "We have sent six shipwrights of whom Robert Moulton is chief."

In another letter on May 28, 1629, they say, "The provisions for building ships, as pitch, tar, rosin, oakum, cordage and sail-cloth in all these ships, with nine firkins and two half-barrels of nails in the *Two Sisters*, are two-thirds for the company and one-third for the Governor, Mr. Cradock."

These letters show conclusively that vessels were built in the settlement prior to the building of the *Blessing of the Bay*, claimed to have been the first built in New England.

As Governor Cradock's location was in Medford, the place where his vessels were built, it is fair to consider the *Rebecca* the older vessel of the two.

Originally published in vol. 11, 1908.

OLD SHIPS AND SHIPBUILDING DAYS OF MEDFORD: 1800–1812
Hall Gleason

Mystic River was an ideal location for shipbuilding. Its serpentine windings from the ocean presented the greatest convenience for a large number of yards. Twice a day the tide surged in from the ocean, mingling its odor of brine with the pungent smell of molasses from the distilleries, and overflowed onto the whispering marshes, making at full tide enough depth of water to float an empty ship of 2,500 tons.

So thought Thatcher Magoun as, strolling one pleasant day to the top of Winter Hill, he stood on one of the mounds of earth that had been thrown up by the Patriot army twenty-seven years before. After a survey of the river "as the tide gave its full outline" like a gigantic lariat below him, he started to interview the captain of a schooner lying at the wharf of one of the distilleries as to the depth and character of the river.

After examining for himself the bed of the river and the depth of water at low tide and finding the neighborhood could furnish an ample supply of oak timber, he finally decided to locate his yard at the spot where all his ships were built. In 1802 was laid the keel of the first of the merchant ships that were known in every sea on the globe.

Thatcher Magoun was born at Pembroke, Massachusetts, on June 17, 1775. He early chose the trade of ship carpenter and served his time with Enos Briggs at Salem, where he worked five years. From Salem he went to Mr. Barker's yard in Charlestown (the present navy yard), where he worked and studied two years and assisted in modeling. There he made the model of the first vessel he built, which was the *Mt. Aetna* of Medford.

Some of Medford's major shipbuilders. James O. Curtis (bottom left), Joshua T. Foster (top left), Thatcher Magoun (center), William M. Cudworth (bottom right) and Foster Waterman (upper right).

Following Mr. Magoun the next year, Calvin Turner of Pembroke and Enos Briggs of the Essex County family of that name built the ship *Medford* of 238 tons for John C. Jones of Boston. After them came Sprague & James, Lapham, Fuller, Rogers, Stetson, Waterman, Ewell, Curtis, Foster, Taylor, Hayden & Cudworth and others who have built vessels here.

After the Revolution, the New England states in particular found themselves in desperate straits from the cutting off of their trade with the West Indies and Great Britain through the operation of the British navigation laws. Finally a scheme for a trade with China was worked out by Boston merchants. This was the sending of vessels to the northwest coast and trading with the Indians for the skins of sea otter, which brought a high price in China for use by the mandarins, and bringing back home or to Europe cargoes of silks, china ware, tea and other eastern goods.

This trade proved immensely profitable. They set out with a cargo composed of chisels made of scraps of iron fitted into rough wooden handles, pieces of copper in squares and brilliant cloths. The total value of ship, outfit and cargo estimated at less than $40,000, and sometimes brought back from China cargoes valued at over $250,000. A number of Medford vessels were engaged in this trade. They were vessels of 200 to 300 tons, permitting their use in the shallow bays of the northwest coast. Among them was the ship *Eclipse*, 343 tons, built for Thomas H. Perkins, James Perkins and James Lloyd in 1805 by T. Magoun.

In 1807 Captain Joseph O'Cain of Boston chartered his ship *Eclipse* of Boston to the Russian-American Company, traded their furs at Canton, visited Nagasaki and Petropavlovsh, lost the vessel on the Aleutian islands, built another out of the wreck and returned to trade once more.

Another Medford-built ship engaged in the northwest fur trade was the brig *Charon*, 238 tons, built in 1890 for P.P. Jackson of Boston by T. Magoun. In 1811, in command of Captain Whittemore, she is mentioned as one of the hunting craft that carried north eighteen hundred skins and was found at the Farallones the next year.

The northwest fur trade was extremely dangerous in the early days. In 1800 the captain of the ship *Globe* was killed by the Indians. The next year, the officers of the ship *Boston* and all but two of the crew were killed by the natives at Nootka Sound. The vessel was afterward accidentally burned.

The dangers were also great from pirates on the China coast. On the evening of August 22, 1809, Captain William Sturgis anchored in Macao Roads. Early the next morning he sent a boat with his first officer and four seamen ashore for a pilot to take his ship up the river to Canton, leaving but ten men on board. Hardly had they started when the vessel was furiously attacked by a fleet of twenty-one pirate junks manned by two thousand men and led by the admiral's junk itself of twenty-eight guns. The pirates attempted to set fire to the ship but were unsuccessful. They then tried to board, but Captain Sturgis, keeping up a hot fire from his six six-pounders, which did fearful execution, cut his cables and succeeded in setting some sail, by which he worked his way over under the guns of the fort.

Many of the first vessels built in Medford were in the Mediterranean trade. They would take a cargo of rum and salt fish to the Southern states or West Indies and carry a cargo of cotton, tobacco and sugar to Europe.

The ship *Medford* is reported in the *Columbian Centinel* as follows:

> *Boston, January 1, 1810. Arrived ship Medford, Capt. J. Barnard, fifty-two days from Cadiz with salt and fruit to J.C. Jones. The Medford on the 4th of October, off Gaskey light, on her passage from London to Cadiz in ballast fell in with and was fired upon by a French privateer of ten guns, the captain of which on hearing she was from an English port, said she was a good prize; but while Captain Barnard was on board the privateer an English lugger hove in sight, when his papers were given up and he permitted to proceed on his voyage. The Frenchmen did not permit themselves time to plunder the Medford but made all sail to get off. The French commander treated Captain Barnard with much civility. The lugger boarded the Medford and informed she had prevented the same privateer from capturing the New Galen, but was not able to capture her, the Frenchman outsailing him.*

The brig *Mt. Aetna*, 188 tons, was the first vessel built in Medford at the yard of Thatcher Magoun. Other Medford-built ships reported at Mediterranean ports in 1810 include the *Commerce* and the *Ariadne* at Cadiz. The *Commerce* sailed from Palermo for Tarragona on April 27, 1810. The ship *Commerce*, 378 tons, was built in 1807 by Calvin Turner for John Holland of Boston. The ship *Ariadne*, 382 tons, was built in 1809 by Calvin Turner for Nathaniel Goddard of Boston.

The brig *Hope*, 160 tons, was built at Medford in 1804 at the yard of Thatcher Magoun for Samuel Gray of Salem. There are several journals of her voyages in the Essex Institute, one a "Log of the brig Hope from Salem to Leghorn. Sailed December 4, 1804, and arrived January 21, 1805, with a cargo of pepper." The following is an entry while at anchor discharging her cargo at Leghorn, describing a gale, February 1, 1805: "Swedish bark went adrift and came down. Bent both parts of the Horses [hawsers] on to the Cables and paid out to the better end and got clear of her."

There were a number of Medford ships in the East India trade at this time. The ship *Gulliver*, built in 1806 by Thatcher Magoun for Joseph Lee

Jr. of Boston, was one. The *Gulliver* is reported February 13, 1810, at the Vineyard as arriving from Calcutta. Her cargo is not given, but other vessels from that port brought indigo, ginger and cotton and silk goods.

Medford shipbuilding started at the height of the prosperity of the northwest trade. The European trade was very profitable, also, owing to the high prices obtained during the Napoleonic wars, in spite of frequent capture and condemnation of vessels. George Cabot said, "Profits were such that if only one out of three vessels escaped capture, her owners could make a handsome profit on the lot." This continued up to the time of the embargo by the Jefferson administration, the outcome of the impressment of seamen of the USS *Chesapeake* on the high seas.

This measure was unpopular in New England and revived the Federalist Party, which had almost ceased to exist. The Federalist leaders ridiculed Jefferson's claim that the embargo was to protect the merchant vessels by calling attention to the fact that the embargo was extended to the East India and China trade, which Great Britain permitted and Napoleon was powerless to prevent. They also claimed that the profits annually on the cargoes were more than equal to the total value of the shipping.

During the embargo of 1808 an inoffensive old schooner came up the Mystic River with her decks piled high with wood and bark. A customhouse officer suspected her of smuggling and took possession of her. The captain invited the officer to dine with him. After a while the captain asked to be excused a few moments to give some orders to the men. As soon as he gained the deck he turned and fastened the cabin door. Stevedores disguised as Indians unloaded the vessel, which had her hold filled with English goods from Halifax. During a large part of the night wagons were taking the contraband merchandise to Boston, Malden and West Cambridge. Her cargo was very valuable. The goods escaped without discovery, but the vessel was confiscated and condemned.

Captain Charles C. Doten of Plymouth, during a northeast gale, slipped by the revenue cutter at Provincetown with the brig *Hope*. He was pursued and fired upon, but escaped to St. Lucia, where he sold the vessel and cargo of fish for $25,000. He brought his Spanish doubloons home sewed into his clothing.

Jefferson signed the repeal of the embargo on his last day in office. Immediately there ensued a tremendous boom in shipping to Mediterranean, Russian and Oriental ports, which continued until the War of 1812.

Originally published in vol. 26, 1923.

Opposite: Medford's final clipper ship *Pilgrim*, in the last stages of construction, 1873.

OLD SHIPS AND SHIPBUILDING DAYS OF MEDFORD: AFTER 1812
Hall Gleason

After the War of 1812, the northwest fur trade gradually declined for various reasons, the gradual extermination of the sea otter and competition by the British and Russians being the principal ones. By this time, cotton manufacturing, encouraged by the embargoes and by the War of 1812, and later by a protective tariff, had increased enormously and a considerable amount was sent to the Far East as cargo.

The *Jones* and the *Tamahourelaune* were built in Medford and sold in Hawaii for sandalwood. *The History of Medford* says they were taken apart and sent out in the *Thaddeus*, but this is probably incorrect, as Morison in an article on the Hawaiian trade gives reliable evidence that they were sailed round. The *Jones* was renamed the *Inore*.

Bryant and Sturgis sent the *Sachem* round to California for a load of hides. This was the beginning of a trade that grew to large proportions and ten or fifteen years later was described so vividly by R.H. Dana in that masterpiece, *Two Years Before the Mast*. The brig *Pilgrim*, in which he went out, was built in Medford and the ship *California* that they helped to load was also. Dana gives the following description of her: "She was a good substantial ship, not quite so long as the *Alert*, wall-sided and kettle-bottomed, after the latest fashion of south shore cotton and sugar wagons, strong too, and tight and a good average sailor, but with no pretensions to beauty and nothing in the style of a 'crack ship.'"

THE PAUL JONES

Between 1830 and 1840 there had been a great improvement in the design of vessels, which greatly increased their speed. Among them was the ship *Paul Jones*, built by Waterman and Ewell at Medford in 1842, of 680 tons, and owned by John M. Forbes of Boston and Russell & Co. of China. She was the perfection of the Medford clipper type of 1830, and the fastest vessel of her time, with the exception of the *Natchez*.

The *Paul Jones* was commanded on her first voyage by N.B. Palmer. Captain Palmer was born in Stonington, Connecticut, on Long Island Sound, in 1799, and came from distinguished colonial ancestry.

On her first voyage the *Paul Jones* in 1843 sailed from Boston for Hong Kong on January 15. She crossed the equator 26 days out, was 54 days to the Cape of Good Hope, 88 days to Java Head and arrived at Hong Kong 111 days from Boston. In 1848 this ship made the run from Java Head to New York in 76 days. Later she was used in the ice carrying trade.

Frederick Tudor, after twenty-eight years of struggle and experimenting, had built up an ice exporting business. After numerous failures, he had by 1812 built up a small trade with the West Indies. The war wiped him out. After the peace of Ghent he obtained government permission to build icehouses at Kingston and Havana, with a monopoly of the traffic. It began to pay, and between 1817 and 1820 he extended the business to Charleston, Savannah and New Orleans. He extended the business to the Far East later,

and the *Paul Jones* carried the first cargo of ice to China. Tudor first shipped ice from his father's pond in Saugus. Later he had icehouses on several of the large ponds nearby, among them one at Spot Pond. People thought he was mad, and seafaring men thought such a cargo would melt and swamp the vessel. It was difficult for him to get a crew. Tudor experimented with various materials for filling—rice and wheat chaff, hay, tan bark and even coal dust—until he finally decided on sawdust.

Clipper ships, 1830–1848

Morison gives the Medford builders a large share of the credit for the improvement in vessels in this period. He says, "The finest type of the period was the Medford or Merrimac-built East Indiaman," and "after 1815, the vessels that he built for the China trade gave Thatcher Magoun a reputation second to none among American ship builders, and 'Medford-built' came to mean the best"; and also, "The Medford builders, in particular, had quietly evolved a new type of four hundred and fifty tons burthen which, handled by eighteen officers and men, would carry half as much freight as a British East Indiaman of fifteen hundred tons with a crew of one hundred and twenty-five and sail half again as fast."

The *Rajah*, built by J. Stetson at Medford in 1836, 530 tons, 140 feet long and 30 feet beam, is cited as a fair specimen of our best freighting vessels.

Deacon Samuel Train, in partnership with his brother Enoch, had built for them the largest vessel up to that time, the *St. Petersburg*. She was built by Waterman & Ewell in 1839, and was 160 feet long, 33 feet broad and 814 tons burthen. She had the painted ports and square stern of a New York packet ship, and had such beautiful fittings and accommodations that she attracted crowds of sightseers at every port. Richard Trask of Manchester, her master and part owner, was one of the dandy merchant captains of his generation. After arranging for the return cargo at St. Petersburg and visiting his friends, he would leave the vessel in charge of the first officer and return via London by steamer.

The word clipper means swift, and the clipper ship is one designed primarily for speed. Although vessels of this type were designed to carry large cargoes, they were so much faster than others of that time that they are usually referred to as the clipper type of 1830.

Originally published in vol. 27, 1924.

Opposite: Ice cutting operation on Spot Pond, 1889.

OLD SHIPS AND SHIPBUILDING DAYS OF MEDFORD: THE CALIFORNIA CLIPPER SHIP ERA
Hall Gleason

The New York builders took the lead in the changes designed to improve the speed of vessels after 1840. Mr. John W. Griffiths, a New York designer, advocated increasing the proportion of length to breadth and sharpening the body fore and aft, with long hollow water lines, and bringing the greatest breadth and center of buoyancy further aft. Another improvement he suggested was to round up the ends of the main transom, thereby relieving the quarters and thus making the after-body finer and the stern above the waterline much lighter and handsomer.

The first vessel built in this part of the country on these ideas was the *Game Cock*, built by Samuel Hall at East Boston in 1850, and the same year James O. Curtis of Medford built the *Shooting Star*—nine hundred tons—for Reed and Wade of Boston. She was one of twenty-six ships that made the passage twice from Boston or New York to San Francisco in less than 110 days average time (105 days from Boston and 115 days from New York, average 110 days).

The other Medford ships in this list are the *Herald of the Morning*, 99 days and 106 days (average 102 days); the *Don Quixote*, 106 days and 108 days

Advertising card for the clipper ship *Eagle Wing*, built by James O. Curtis.

(average 107 days); and the *Ringleader*, 107 days and 110 days (average 108½ days). There was but one Medford ship, the *Herald of the Morning*, out of the eighteen that made the passage to San Francisco in less than 100 days. Yet in proportion to the number built, the Medford clipper ships made more fast records than the average. The *Herald of the Morning* made the trip in 99 days from New York. She was designed by Samuel A. Pook of Boston, who also designed the *Ocean Telegraph*, built by James O. Curtis in 1854. Other famous ships designed by Mr. Pook were the *Red Jacket* and *Game Cock*.

Captain Clark mentions 23 Medford ships in a list of 173 extreme type of clipper ships built between 1850 and 1857. In a record of 128 passages made to San Francisco in 110 days or less between 1850 and 1860, from New York or Boston, 17 were made by 13 Medford ships as follows:

Ship	**Days**	**Port of Departure**	**Date of Arrival**
Courser	108	Boston	April 28, 1852
Don Quixote	106	Boston	March 29, 1855
Eagle Wing	105	Boston	April 5, 1854
Electric Spark	106	Boston	April 9, 1856
Golden Eagle	105	Boston	August 25, 1854
Herald of the Morning	106	Boston	May 7, 1854
Herald of the Morning	99	New York	May 16, 1855
Ocean Telegraph	109	New York	March 13, 1860
Phantom	105	Boston	April 21, 1853
Ringleader	110	Boston	February 8, 1854
Ringleader	107	Boston	February 12, 1856
Robin Hood	107	New York	March 25, 1859
Shooting Star	105	Boston	August 17, 1852
Telegraph	109	Boston	April 9, 1855
White Swallow	110	New York	August 7, 1860

Of the remainder of the twenty-three ships mentioned by Captain Clark, the following passages are recorded from Boston or New York to San Francisco: *Dauntless*, 116 days; *John Wade*, 116 days; *Kingfisher*, 114 days; *Fleetwing*, 121 days; *Norwester*, 122 days; *Morning Star*, 146 days; *Syren*, 118 days.

Other ships of this period, but not in this list of extreme clipper type, which made fast voyages to San Francisco from Boston or New York were the *National Eagle*, 134 days; *Wild Ranger*, 122 and 127 days; *Osborn Howes*, 153 days; and *Good Hope*, 143 days. The *Thatcher Magoun* made the trip from San Francisco to New York in 94 days.

Originally published in vol. 28, 1925.

Advertisement for the clipper ship *Syren*, built by John Taylor.

Old Ship Street: Some of its Houses, Ships and Characters
Fred H.C. Woolley

When Thatcher Magoun, of Pembroke, Massachusetts, came to Medford, and in 1802 selected a portion of land between the river and this road opposite its junction with Park Street, and here located the first shipyard, an industry started that drew to Medford in the succeeding years many men and their families who located their homes along this road. These men came mainly from Scituate, Marshfield, Hanover and Pembroke, where for years shipbuilding had flourished, finding here better facilities for their chosen occupation. And so it came about that soon afterward a name was given to this street that seemed exactly fitting; for at a town meeting held May 4, 1829, a committee that had been appointed to recommend names for the streets reported as follows: "From Porter's corner southeast to Wellington farm, Ship Street." Unfortunately after fifty years the name "Ship Street" was laid aside on petition of the last shipbuilder of the Ship Street yards. Perhaps it seemed to him an appropriate thing to do, as shipbuilding was then in its decline in Medford, and it happened that he built the last ship. On November 15, 1872, it was voted at town meeting that the name of Ship Street be changed to Riverside Avenue, on petition of J.T. Foster and others.

Houses and Characters

The men who came to Medford to engage in the shipbuilding industry and settled along Ship Street built plain, substantial houses of ample proportion varying but little in style from one another. The square pitch roof with one large chimney in the center, or a chimney at each end, was the predominant type. A few gambrel-roofed houses are still to be seen, but none of the hip-roofed type, of which there were three, are in existence. These houses, backed by orchards, fronted by the sturdy lilacs, guarded by sentinel posts at the front gateway of the picket fence, shaded by chestnut, buttonwoods or elms, were the pride of those shipbuilders and carpenters. There many of the substantial citizens of Medford grew up.

Mr. Thatcher Magoun, the pioneer shipbuilder, built his residence at the easterly corner of Park and Ship Streets, a large two-and-a-half-story house, hip-roofed, with a long L and a barn somewhat back with a curving driveway thereto. Several large elms in later days shaded the place.

An artist's view of Ship Street as it may have looked during Medford's shipbuilding days.

Here a great many of those who afterward became shipbuilders boarded while serving their apprenticeship with Mr. Magoun. His shipyard was opposite, where from 1803, the year of the launching of his first vessel, the *Mt. Aetna*, until he launched his last, the *Deucalion*, in 1836, he built more than any other one builder in Medford, his list of vessels numbering eighty-four. He finally removed to the residence he built on High Street (now the public library). On September 19, 1865, his old home, then occupied by several families as a tenement house, was completely burned.

Mr. Calvin Turner, who established the second shipyard at the corner of Cross and Ship Streets, in 1805 lived in a house similar in build to Mr. Magoun's. It was situated near where the present Boston & Maine freight shed stands, but was moved to Court Street some years ago. Mr. Turner was esteemed a faithful builder, and is to be credited with twenty-five vessels.

Another contemporary was Samuel Lapham, son of George Bryant Lapham of Marshfield, Massachusetts, who came here in 1800 and built his homestead on Ship Street, some distance below Park Street and nearly opposite what is now Maverick Street. Here was born, on November 4, 1808, Samuel Lapham II, who became apprenticed to Thatcher Magoun and, after serving his time, started business on his own account. He built his first vessel, the brig *Nabob*, in 1830, at which time he purchased the yards and residence at the corner of Cross and Ship Streets. The ship *Magnet*, his twenty-third vessel and launched in 1856, was the last vessel built by him or in his yards. He then retired from the business of building vessels, in most of which he was part or sole owner. He built several ships—the *Argonaut*, *Don Quixote* and others—for Mr. John E. Lodge, the father of Senator Henry Cabot Lodge.

Of all the homesteads on old Ship Street, that of Mr. Galen James (Deacon James) stands out clearest in memory, situated at the corner of what is now known as Foster Court. It was imposing; a large brown house, a long, low ell connected with shed, carriage house and barn of ample proportion shaded by large elms.

Mr. James, born in Scituate in 1790, came to Medford in the early years of 1800 and learned the shipbuilding trade of Thatcher Magoun, in whose family he lived while so doing. He built his house in 1820. He formed a partnership with Mr. Isaac Sprague and they started a shipyard in 1817, the third in Medford, at the foot of what is now Foster Court. Their first vessel was built in 1816, named the *Bocca Tigris*; the last was built in 1842, the bark *Altorf*. Several of their vessels were built for Mr. Joseph Lee of Boston, a bachelor of eccentric character.

Mr. Isaac Sprague, the partner of Mr. James, came to Medford from Scituate and bought the house now known as the old Sprague House, situated near Spring Street. This house had only two rooms in the main

The home of shipbuilder Galen James. The house was in the Italianate style popular in the 1860s.

part, but was from time to time enlarged until it assumed goodly proportions. The barn was built by Mr. Sprague, at the raising of which many of the neighbors helped. Here he kept the oxen that he used in the shipyard for hauling timber. Mr. William Sprague and Mr. Isaac Sprague, his sons, still live in Medford. He died January 12, 1852, age sixty-nine years.

A low one-story house with large chimney and sloping roof, nestled amid lilacs and bright flowers, is remembered as the home of Mr. Nathan Sawyer, just this side of Mr. Sprague's. He came to Medford in 1827 and in 1836 bought this house of a Mrs. Hatch, living here until he died in 1873. He had charge of making all the ironwork used by Sprague & James in the building of their ships, and owned two or three shops, having many men to work for him.

The white house with cupola built by Mr. C.S. Jacobs, back from the street among the trees, with the long iron fence front, and opposite the old Sprague homestead, is known as the home of Mr. Joshua T. Foster, proprietor of the last shipyard. He came to Medford from South Scituate in 1826 and served with Sprague & James. In 1852 he became partner with Mr. John Taylor, succeeding his old employers. Afterward he became sole owner of the yard, where, until he launched his last in 1873, he built some famous vessels—forty-two in all. He was captain of the Medford militia in 1834, and held many offices in the town, being for eleven years a selectman and four years an assessor. In 1883–84 he represented Medford in the legislature. He died November 21, 1895.

The home of ship ironworker Nathan Sawyer, who lived in the house from 1836 to 1873.

We have now sauntered slowly down old Ship Street from the home of the pioneer shipbuilder at the corner of Park Street. We have stood in front of the homes or the sites of the homes of those men who made Medford ships famous, and in memory they have lived again. Turning now westward from Park Street, other homes and persons come to mind that had their part in this important industry.

At the upper corner of Pleasant Street was the house of Mr. William Cudworth, who, in partnership with Mr. Elisha Hayden, was the last to carry on shipbuilding at the old Magoun yard. Both these men came from Scituate, Mr. Cudworth being born January 15, 1814, at a place now called Greenbush. His schooling was cut short at the age of thirteen, when he was sent to sea (his father being a captain) to help in support of the family. From his youth he loved ships, and it is said he used to draw and cut upon the panels of the rooms of his early home pictures of vessels in varied rig. Hayden & Cudworth built their first ship—the *Horsburgh*, 577 tons—in 1846; their largest and last—the *Henry Hastings*, 1,500 tons—in 1866; in all thirty-nine vessels. Mr. Cudworth served the town of Medford as one of its selectmen several times and was a representative to the legislature for three consecutive sessions. He died at his home on February 2, 1877.

SOME OF ITS SHIPS

The ship *Gem of the Ocean*, 730 tons, built by Hayden & Cudworth, was launched at midnight, August 4, 1852, on account of the tide. Each man brought his lantern. Mr. Cudworth's mother, then seventy years of age, never having witnessed a launch, came up from Scituate and was present at the event—a great one for her.

The ship *Electric Spark*, 1,200 tons, launched at the same yard in 1855, was commanded by Captain R.G.F. Candage (now of Brookline) and made the voyage to California in 106 days.

The *Boston Advertiser* of Saturday, May 10, 1856, had the following advertisement:

> *Glidden & Williams line for San Francisco*
> *To Sail on or before Tuesday, May 20,*
> *the Magnificent first-Class Clipper Ship Thatcher Magoun*
> *S.B. Bourne, Comdr.*
> *The Thatcher Magoun is truly an elegant ship extremely sharp and ventilated in the most thorough manner. She will sail as above.*
> *For Freight or Passage*

Apply at California Packet office
39 Lewis Wharf.

She was built by Hayden and Cudworth.

The ship *Don Quixote*, built at Foster's yard in 1868, had a notice in the *Boston Evening Journal* of October 29, 1868, as follows: "Launched, ship *Don Quixote*. A fine vessel of about 1,000 tons was launched by Mr. Foster, at Medford, a few days since. She now lies at Long wharf and will load for San Francisco." Her commander was Captain Nelson, formerly of the ship *Golden Fleece*, and she sailed for Winsor's regular line for San Francisco.

The ship *Pilgrim*—long may she be remembered as the last of all the vessels built and launched on the shores of the Mystic! She was constructed at J.T. Foster's yard for Henry Hastings & Co. Of nearly a thousand tons, launched on December 3, 1873, she sailed to Hong Kong February 14, 1874, with a cargo of ice, and was commanded by Captain Frank Fowle, making the passage in 121 days. Afterward, in December 1889, she was sold to Daniel Bacon of New York. She was constructed of the finest material, sailed the world over making fair passages and was eventually lost.

Passengers and Captain R.F.D. Candage (second from the left) on board the *Electric Spark* in 1865. The ship was built by Hayden and Cudworth.

SHIPBUILDING

In the early days of shipbuilding, work in the yards began with sunrise and ended at sunset, with allowance of time for meals. In later times the work hours were from seven in the morning until six at night with an hour's nooning. Usually about sixty men were employed building a ship. They were the ship carpenters, the caulkers and the outboard and inboard joiners. The wages received were two dollars per day, apprentices receiving forty to fifty dollars per year and board; many of the apprentices boarded with the proprietor of the yard. To build a 1,000- or 1,200-ton ship required about six months. In early times the timber was obtained in the neighborhood, and later in New Hampshire, from where it was transported via the old Middlesex Canal to Medford and drawn by ox teams to the shipyard. It was a sight in winter to see these teams go by—creaking, squeaking, the oxen with frosted backs and icicles hanging from their mouths.

To be in the yard watching the varied processes going on in the ship's construction was the acme of delight to the interested boy. Oftentimes a few pennies were earned by some errand or by tending the steam-shed fire. "Looking in at the open door" of the blacksmith shop never lacked in attraction for the children. In early days matches were unknown, and old Mr. Lapham, the blacksmith, would be seen daily coming up the street from his house with his firebrand to light his forge fire. What a supply of "chewing gum" for the children there was in those big kettles of tar, where all were permitted to help themselves without spending a cent!

The great day was the day of the launch. The neighborhood poured out—old ship captains came from far and near—the "school-marm" and her flock of boys and girls. It was a sight—grand, impressive to look at the great ship that had been building so many months, now awaiting, in her dress of black and green, the incoming tide, when, the last block knocked from under, she would slide into the Mystic.

Of all the buildings in all the yards but one stands today—an old building in Foster's yard. A slight depression nearby on the edge of the river marks the spot where the last ship was launched—the *Pilgrim*. The tides come and go as they always have. Old Ship Street with its ships has passed into history. No shipbuilder is now living. Their sons and daughters are still with us.

Originally published in vol. 4, 1901.

The skeleton of a ship under construction in the Curtis shipyard.

The launching of the *Pilgrim* from Foster's wharf on December 4, 1873.

Chapter 4

SLAVERY AND THE CIVIL WAR

SLAVERY IN MEDFORD
Walter H. Cushing

Slavery existed in Massachusetts almost from the first settlement of the colony, and was somewhat increased as a result of the Pequot war in 1637. The slaves in this instance were, of course, Indians. The chief source of African slaves, so far as their importation is concerned, was through trade with Barbados, a British island in the West Indies. Slaves purchased in Africa were sold chiefly in the West Indies and the Southern colonies; the balance came north.

The mainspring of the traffic was rum, and Brooks in his *History of Medford* gives an extract from a captain's account book showing balance between rum and slaves.

In proportion to its size Medford seems to have had a large number of slaves. Out of 114 towns returning the number of Negro slaves, Medford ranks twelfth. In 1755 the number of slaves sixteen years old and upward was thirty-four, of whom twenty-seven were males. There was no return from Charlestown; but the only other town in Middlesex County returning a larger number was Cambridge, which reported a total of fifty-six.

One of the most valuable bits of statistics relating to Medford, however, is contained in the *Columbian Centinel* of August 17, 1822. It is entitled an "Account of the Houses, Families, Number of White People, Negroes & Indians, in the Province of Mass. Bay, taken in the year 1764 and 1765."

GLIMPSES OF MEDFORD: SELECTIONS FROM THE HISTORICAL REGISTER

Evidently a census had been undertaken and, as such inquiries were notoriously unpopular, it was either unfinished or at least not published. A copy of it came into the possession of the *Centinel* and was published as an interesting source of local history. That portion relating to Medford is here given in full:

Houses	Families	Males under 16	Females under 16	Males over 16	Females over 16	Negroes	Total
104	147	161	150	207	223	49	790

The Negroes thus constituted one-sixteenth of the population of the town in 1765. By way of comparison it may be added that in 1822 Medford had 1,474 inhabitants; in fifty-seven years it had failed to double its population. As the ratio of whites to blacks in the colony at large was forty-five to one, it is seen that Medford had an unusually large Negro population. So far as I have found records, a strong, able-bodied Negro was worth, in 1700, about eighteen pounds. In the inventory of Major Jonathan Wade's property appears the following asset: "5 negros £97," and elsewhere in his papers is the record: "2 negroes that died appraised @ £35." Still, it is impossible to generalize from such insufficient data. After the beginning of hostilities in 1775 Colonel Royall departed for Nova Scotia, and Dr. Tufts for a while managed his property. Under date of March 12, 1776, Royall writes,

> *Please to sell the following negroes; Stephen and George; they each cost £60 sterling; and I would take £50, or even £15, apiece for them. Hagar cost £35 sterling, but I will take £30 for her. I gave for Mira £35, but will take £25. If Mr. Benjamin Hall will give the £100 for her which he offered, he may have her, it being a good place. As to Betsey and her daughter Nancy, the former may tarry, or take her freedom, as she may choose; and Nancy you may put out to some good family by the year.*

The range of prices is here much higher, averaging about £40.

The records of vital statistics contain frequent notices of slaves. Of these the most numerous are the deaths; the fewest are the marriages. As the master's name is given in many cases, these records also throw light on the question of slaveholders in Medford. About forty deaths are recorded between 1745 and 1780. It is rather curious that three of Colonel Royall's slaves died within a year, at the outbreak of the Revolution. Perhaps they were heartbroken at his departure. A few entries are given here by way of illustration:

Peter, Son of Worcester & Flora, Negroes of Rev. Mr. Turell and Stephen Hall, Esq., Died Jan. 9, 1762.

Plato, a Negro Servant of Hon. Isaac Royall Esq., drowned June 8, 1768.

London, A Negro Man of the Widow Mary Bradshaw's Died Oct. 15, 1760.

Caesar, Negro Servant of Ebenezar Brooks of Medford and Zipporah negro Servant of Nathl Brown of Charlestown, married June 23, 1757.

As would be inferred, the number of slave owners was not large, and they were the leading men of the town: the Halls, Brookses and Willises, Dr. Simon Tufts, Reverend Mr. Turrell and, above all, Colonel Isaac Royall. This first Royall brought with him from Antigua a number of slaves and in 1737 petitioned that the duty on them be abated, but no further action was taken than to lay it on the table. He probably had at least fifteen at a time, and the slave-quarters, so-called, have become an object of considerable historical interest. The entire number of persons holding slaves in the last half of the eighteenth century probably did not exceed thirty, the town records giving, indirectly, the names of twenty. Not that our ancestors believed it wrong; the names of Reverend Mr. Turrell and Deacon Benjamin Willis would refute that. But economically it was unprofitable, and its ultimate extinction was doubtless the expectation of all who gave the subject any thought.

The Isaac Royall House and slave quarters.

I have set forth, with little comment, the few brief facts relating to slavery in our town. Perhaps, on the whole, it is a matter of congratulation that the facts are so meager. "Happy is the people whose annals are uninteresting!"

Originally published in vol. 3, 1900.

SOME LETTERS OF MISS LUCY OSGOOD
Reverend Henry C. Delong

Miss Lucy Osgood, some of whose letters I have the privilege of presenting, was the second daughter of David Osgood, DD, who was the honored minister of Medford from 1774 to 1822, a period of forty-eight years. She was born June 17, 1791, and died on her eighty-second birthday, June 17, 1873. So far as I can learn the education of the daughters of Dr. Osgood, after their early years, was received wholly from himself. Miss Lucy, as well as her older sister Mary, was instructed by her father in Hebrew, Greek and Latin, and in Greek and Latin she was proficient and was the equal of college professors who, during her father's life, were frequent visitors at his house.

The David Osgood House, also home to his daughter Lucy, on the corner of Powderhouse Road and High Street.

All through her letters I am struck with her vital interest in whatever concerns the morals of society. She was a little late in espousing the antislavery cause, and was led to it by the prodding of her friend, Lydia Maria Child, but her acceptance of it was wholehearted. The letters were just previous to the War of the Rebellion, and while it continued, show the warmest interest, are filled with love of country and of the freedom of the slave that the dread ordeal must establish.

In these letters may be traced the history of Miss Osgood, her scholarly, literary, moral, philanthropic and religious interests, as well as her personal characteristics. Only a small portion of them can be presented from lack of space to print them. But it is good to preserve some clear outline of this noble and gifted woman, who was honored and beloved in Medford, and is worthy of the remembrance of a later generation, to win it, if it may be, "to the still air of delightful studies."

Mrs. John Brown
Letter, September 15, 1856

I wish to give you an account of a most interesting guest who was with us last evening. Mrs. Holman came in bringing with her a lady whom she introduced to me as a Mrs. Brown just arrived from Kansas where her husband, the editor of the Herald of Freedom, *is now imprisoned with Gov. Robinson and his companions. We gazed upon her with interest. She was a superb looking woman, six feet high at the least, from thirty-three to thirty-eight years old apparently; not a mother, but the partner of all her husband's labors and dangers. She had learned the use of fire-arms, and could defend herself with muskets, revolvers or pistols. She had gone from Pennsylvania to Kansas two years or more since with three hundred other emigrants, and the implements for a large printing establishment which was in successful operation when the Missouri ruffians demolished it. She had ventured alone from Kansas to St. Louis by the river route in a boat lined with the ruffians, who held her in suspicion and endeavored in every way to detect her business and objects. Though entrusted with important despatches she succeeded in baffling their curiosity, and proceeded to her main object, which was to obtain from some of the U.S. Judges a habeas corpus act for the release of her husband. In part of her mission she had failed; all with one consent having found some excuse for evading her just demand. She is now impatiently waiting for an opportunity to return; and to the inquiry, what were her prospects? modestly but firmly replied, "Whether my husband lives or dies, his paper will be carried on; I shall edit it in his absence." She was brought here last evening by Mr. Andrew, a lawyer from Boston, who was to address our Fremont Club, and supposing that it might be attended here as in so many other places by the women, he had invited this lady to accompany him and tell her story, so that we had the benefit of hearing what she had expected to relate to the public. Her narrative was absolutely thrilling; she described one night in which she and her husband were watched by an armed band of ruffians, who not content with thrusting their heads into the room through an open window, finally broke open the door which was fastened on the inside, and marched round the bed. "I lifted myself up," said the six foot lady, "and bowed over my husband, determined that they should assail me first." Last autumn during the week that should have been devoted to gathering in the harvest and preparing for winter, these poor settlers were defending their lives and property against eight hundred Missourians who poured in upon them to control the election, and the consequent suffering during the long hard winter could hardly, she said, be imagined. This morning I have been perambulating our town inviting the good women and true to put their fingers to the work of preparing a box of warm garments to be forwarded to a Boston committee which pledges itself that whatever is committed to them for the benefit of the champions of liberty shall safely reach its destination. Our visitor was sanguine in the expectation that the present reign of iniquity will soon come to an end. I can only say, "God grant it may."*

ANTISLAVERY DAYS
LETTER, JUNE 18, 1854

I went to Boston on Sunday to hear Theodore Parker. We had a little chat with him after service, and asked him his opinion of the state of things. He thinks that what we see is but the beginning of worse to come, and that blood will flow at the next attempt to arrest a fugitive in Boston. Nothing astonishes me so much as the miserable stupidity of the people. They seem to lack the faculty to discern any difference between rebelling against a law which compels them to sin and a vulgar riot designed for the perpetration of deeds of lawlessness. I went twice for a few hours at a time to the city during anniversary week, and heard "the mob, the mob," so often spoken of in tones of disgust and horror, that at last I stood up on the defensive and constantly retorted, "The mob is on my side, I belong to it." I did meet with one funny adventure. When I left the cars my feeling was that I could not for the world pass through Court Square and see the barricaded temple of Justice; but on the same principle I suppose, that people are drawn to look at executions, I had an impulse on returning home to go through the street which I had so sedulously avoided a few hours before. A gentleman pulled me by the sleeve just as I had entered it. "Where now?" said he. "To liberate yonder prisoner" said I. "I wish you Godspeed," he called after me. After a few steps more a lady plucked my shawl, one of the noble Boston women. I stopped to speak with her but she soon interrupted me with, "You must fall into our rank or the police will order you off the sidewalk." As I looked more attentively I perceived that she was standing with her back leaning against the wall of the shops directly opposite the Court House, on the other side of the street, and a long row of women on each side of her were her companions. "Rank?" repeated I, "What are you doing here?" "Bearing our protest!" was her answer. "How? by looking at the Court House!" "We hiss every soldier, and wish all the women to do the same." I confess this mode of protest struck me as irresistibly comic. But it was a real fact, and by night these good ladies were completely spent. Yet how much better this was than the applause and thanks paid by many to the military.

Originally published in vol. 10, 1907.

THE LAWRENCE LIGHT GUARD
Helen Tilden Wild

The military company of Winchester "went off" to Medford and formed the Lawrence Light Guard. The company was organized March 27, 1851, with Frederick O. Prince, afterward mayor of Boston, as captain.

At this time a military company was projected in Medford, and instead of applying for a new charter, Medford men enlisted in the Winchester company with the purpose of reorganizing and transferring the command to Medford. The name was changed to Lawrence Light Guard, in honor of Mr. Daniel Lawrence, who as long as he lived showed his interest by substantial aid.

In the fall of 1860, the political sky was so darkened that there was increased activity in all military organizations. The Light Guard drilled twice a week. In February 1861, the company was called upon to answer the question of whether or not it was ready to respond to a call for troops at a minute's notice. At roll call thirty-eight men answered "yes" and three answered "no." Lieutenant Chambers sent his assent in writing.

Company election was held February 12, 1861, to choose a second lieutenant, and thereafter until the close of the three months' campaign, the officers were: John Hutchins, captain; John G. Chambers, first lieutenant; Perry Colman, second lieutenant; and William H. Pattee, third lieutenant.

Captain John Hutchins.

In March 1861, regimental drills were begun, which were held regularly until the beginning of the war in Fitchburg Hall, Boston. On April 12, 1861, Fort Sumter was fired upon, and on April 15 the "fiery cross" was sent out over the Commonwealth.

Colonel Lawrence was ordered to report in Boston with his regiment on April 19, 1861. His orders were issued April 18, and were delivered by the hand of his brother, Mr. Daniel W. Lawrence. It is a strange coincidence that this second summons of the Minutemen should have come on the exact anniversary of Paul Revere's ride.

On the afternoon of April 20 a great crowd assembled in the square to bid the company Godspeed. A hush fell as the company formed in a hollow square, and the Reverend Jarvis A. Ames of the Methodist church offered prayer. The company left on the two o'clock train, reported for duty on Boston Common at three and thence marched to Faneuil Hall, where they were quartered until the morning of April 21.

They were mustered into the Federal service on May 1, 1861. The enemy had not been seen, but there was, every day, the possibility that something exciting might happen. July 16, 1861, the Light Guard was ordered to march with the army toward Richmond. Sunday morning, July 21, they left Centreville for Bull Run, and then something did happen.

The opposing forces met. By the middle of the afternoon the Union troops seemed on the point of victory, but the arrival of Kirby Smith turned the scale. The Zouaves who were in front broke and retreated in disorder through the Union lines, closely pursued by the Confederates. All the Union men did not wear the regulation United States blue, and many Confederates wore the uniforms of their local organizations. In the confusion, friend could not be distinguished from foe. Rout was inevitable.

In the retreat, Colonel Lawrence was wounded, but in spite of this and the general panic, the Fifth maintained its formation and Captain Hutchins reports that fully three-fourths of his command marched back to camp in regular order. Captain Hutchins's telegram, sent the next morning, allayed the fears of those at home, but the Light Guard was not unscathed. On the night before the battle, Billy Lawrence, the color-bearer, said to a brother sergeant, "We are going into action tomorrow, and as sure as the sun rises, I shall be killed. I shall not put the brass eagle on the staff, but in my haversack. That flag is going to the front tomorrow, and whatever happens to me, don't let the Rebels get it." His presentiment was verified; while carrying the flag in the front line, a bullet pierced his heart. The flag he so bravely carried was saved from capture and is a precious treasure, for it bears the stain of his blood. Manville Richards was wounded in this battle, but recovered and came home to be killed at a fire in Medford a few months later. William Crooker was also wounded and J. Henry Hoyt was taken prisoner.

The three months' term having expired, the Fifth started at once from Alexandria to Washington after the battle. The company arrived in Boston on July 30. They were escorted home by citizens of Medford and the fire companies of the town. The procession was headed by a band of music. On the following Tuesday a formal reception was given them at Child's Grove on Fulton Street. Lieutenant John G. Chambers was commissioned adjutant of the Twenty-third Regiment, October 11, 1861.

In July 1862, Captain Hutchins was appointed major and resigned the command of the Light Guard, being succeeded by Lieutenant Perry Coleman. This arrangement lasted for a very short time, for before the month ended, a letter from the selectmen, desiring the company's services as part of the quota demanded from Medford, had been received and accepted. The first new man to enlist was James A. Hervey. Major Hutchins was made recruiting officer. By August 15, eighty-five members were enrolled. Street drills were held and "High Private" Samuel C. Lawrence took personal charge of the awkward squad. The day fixed for departure was August 25, 1862, and the ceremonies were similar to those of 1861. The minister of the Unitarian church offered prayer and Thomas S. Harlow, Esquire, made an address. The company went first to Lynnfield and then to Boxford, where the Thirty-ninth Regiment was organized. The Light Guard became Company C. The colonel was P.S. Davis.

The Thirty-ninth Regiment left Boxford on September 5, 1862. Immediately upon their arrival in the South, they were put on picket duty on the Potomac River. Writing from Conrad's Ferry, Maryland, on September 20, Captain Hutchins said, "We have slept under a tent but one night since we left Massachusetts." The next morning after arriving at Washington, the regiment marched to Camp Chase at Arlington Heights. They camped there two nights (the second, in tents). The next day was spent on the march, the second in felling trees for a new camp and the night on picket duty. With one day for rest and preparation, they started off on a long march to Ball's Bluff, where six companies were on picket, Captain Hutchins being in command of three of them.

At this time the Light Guard was without change of clothing, their baggage having been left behind when they left Arlington Heights, but Captain Hutchins wrote, "We have two towels and some soap, and the Potomac runs near us." December 20, 1862, after serving all the fall on picket and as river guard, the regiment went into winter quarters at Poolesville. Tents were supplied with bunks and straw. April 14, 1863, marching orders were received. A week later, the Thirty-ninth was in barracks at Washington, D.C., acting as provost guard. From April to July our company enjoyed the pleasure of renewing old friendships and doing easy work. July 12, 1863, just after the battle of Gettysburg, the regiment marched to Funktown, Maryland, and joined the Army of the Potomac under General Meade. The Rappahannock was reached July 27.

General Samuel Crocker Lawrence.

December 2 the corps crossed the Rapidan, the Thirty-ninth being the last to go over. On this march, Charles Coolidge and Henry Currell, being unable to keep up with the column, were captured and died in Libby Prison. December 24, after bivouacking by day and marching by night, the regiment reached the extreme outpost of the army, picketing the northern bank of the Rapidan.

Fighting by day, marching by night, under the indomitable command of Grant, the Army of the Potomac marched through the wilderness. On May 4 the terrible battle began, and for thirty-eight days the army had no sleep except naps on the ground when they halted. The Light Guard lost eighteen men, killed and wounded, in the wilderness. The company was not actually engaged until the fourth day of the engagement at Laurel Hill.

The regiment, charging with fixed bayonets, drove cavalry and then a battery before it, but meeting strongly entrenched infantry, it was forced to fall back over an open field. Here the Light Guard suffered severely. Henry Hathaway, Stephen Busha and Alfred Joyce were missing. The latter died in prison at Andersonville; the others were never heard from. Corporal Stimpson was maimed for life and Sergeants Turner and Morrison were slightly wounded. On May 10 the regiment was in the front line (where it was placed almost without exception all through this campaign). It made no actual demonstration but was exposed to artillery fire. On that day Sergeant Stevens, who had been recommended for promotion, and Privates Bierne and Harding were instantly killed.

On May 12, while the Thirty-ninth filled a gap between the Fifth and Sixth Corps, Edward Ireland was killed and Henry A. Ireland was wounded. On the night of May 13, the command marched through deep mud and pitchy darkness to Spotsylvania, and remained there exposed to the fire of the enemy for a week, when the line was abandoned, leaving pickets to follow. Robert Livingstone of Company C, one of these pickets, was taken prisoner and died at Andersonville.

The Light Guard had its share in the victory that followed the crossing of the North Anna, and the march was continued with constant skirmishing until the fifth of June, when a halt of five days was made at Cold Harbor. The march was resumed June 12 at five o'clock in the afternoon and continued all night, with long halts. The next day the enemy was met at White Oak Swamp, where a line was formed and held until dark, when the corps pushed on to join the main army. After daily skirmishes and nightly marches the column arrived before Petersburg and drove the enemy into its inner works. Here Company C received several additions from recruits of the Twelfth and Thirteenth Massachusetts, whose terms of enlistment had not expired with the mustering out of their regiments.

The Light Guard, with its regiment, was stationed behind entrenchments so exposed that relieving of pickets, drawing rations and ammunition and other necessary work had to be done at night. Joel M. Fletcher's life was sacrificed here. July 11, 1864, Colonel Davis was killed. The order book of the regiment is enough to tell of his character. Captain Hutchins said of him, "The regiment…is the pride of our noble colonel, who is a father to us all, and the best colonel now in the service."

The regiment went into Fort Davis on the day after the colonel's death and remained there until August 18, when it was ordered to destroy the tracks of the Weldon Railroad. A detachment was ordered to tear up the tracks, and another was placed on guard. Suddenly they found themselves surrounded by the enemy. The regiment, besides killed and wounded, lost 245 men. Rodney Hathaway of Company C was killed. Captain Hutchins, Sergeant Eames, Frank J. Curtis, Edwin Ireland, Patrick Gleason, Benjamin J. Ellis, Milton F. Roberts, I.T. Morrison and Lieutenant Hosea of the Light Guard proper, besides several others who had been recruited in Medford, including William H. Rogers, a native of the town, and nine men transferred to Company C from the Twelfth and Thirteenth Massachusetts were taken prisoners. They were first stripped of everything of value and then sent to Richmond, where they were confined in Libby Prison. Although the place was foul and the food bad enough, they were under cover and the rations were cooked. But the nine days of confinement there during midsummer were so hard to bear that they hailed the change to Belle Isle, where they would be sure of air to breathe, but every change brought added discomfort. In October they were transferred to Salisbury, where, without shelter, without cooked food, with hardly water enough to drink and none for bathing, with only vermin-infested rags for covering, they spent a horrible winter. Here Gleason and Rogers died, and the rest looking with hollow eyes into one another's faces gave parting messages for dear ones at home, fearing that a few days more would bring mental or physical death. Deliverance came soon enough to allow Benjamin Ellis and Augustus Tufts to come home to die. One by one these prisoners have dropped out of life since the war, and now Captain Hutchins, J. Henry Eames and Milton F. Roberts are the only ones who can tell that dreadful tale of living death.

On August 21, the Confederates tried for the last time to recover Weldon Railroad. At Hatcher's Run, October 29, Sergeant Edwin B. Hatch of the Light Guard was killed. During December 1864, five men were transferred from Company C to other posts of duty. At that time the regiment was so depleted that the state colors were sent home, there not being enough men to protect two flags. On February 3, Second Lieutenant William McDevitt of Woburn was transferred from Company K and placed in command of the remnant of Company C, and continued until the surrender of Lee, when Captain Hutchins returned to the company. March 29 the spring campaign opened. The Thirty-ninth were sent out as skirmishers, but were driven back, leaving dead and wounded behind. Aaron Tucker and George Graves were taken prisoners in this engagement at Gravelly Run, but were recaptured in a few days.

The Lawrence Light Guard readied for departure, September 23, 1862.

April 1, at Five Forks, the Thirty-ninth was brigaded with Sheridan's cavalry. At noon the line was formed with infantry in the center and cavalry on the flanks. The fight was quick and spirited, and as the Union forces advanced, the evidences of hurried retreat gave them renewed courage. The next day Lieutenant McDevitt and his 12 men, who were the remnant of Company C, took up the march that was to terminate at Appomattox and victory. Of the 101 men who left Medford in August 1862, only 9 took part in the concluding battle as members of Company C. Of these, only Royall S. Carr, Henry A. Ireland, Emery Ramsdell and Edwin F. Kenrick were members of the original Light Guard that had volunteered its services to the selectmen on July 30, 1863. The regiment, after Lee's surrender, marched back toward Petersburg, and on April 21 made camp at Black's and White's station, where many officers and men, paroled prisoners, joined their commands.

May 9 the regiment crossed the Rappahannock for the tenth and last time, as it marched toward Washington and home. The regiment arrived in Readville, Massachusetts, at seven o'clock on the morning of June 6, 1865. The records of the company are responsible for the statement that here the Light Guard, after thirty-four months of faithful service, basely deserted! Nobody blamed them then, and certainly no one does now, for what mortal man could stand being cooped up in barracks, only a few miles from home, which he had not seen for almost three years? But all went back again, and on June 9 appeared at the Providence Station in Boston. After a march through Boston the company took the train to Medford. The arrival of the train at Park Street was announced by the booming of cannon, which was echoed by several other pieces stationed in different parts of the town. The records say, "By their incessant roar they seemed determined to remind us of the many trying scenes through which we had so recently passed." After a march through several of the principal streets to West Medford, where a collation was furnished by the citizens of that part of the town, the company returned to the square, where they were entertained by the Lawrence Rifles at their armory in Usher's Building. The town gave the Light Guard a reception on June 14, and another was given by Washington Engine Company No. 3 at Green Mountain Grove on the twenty-eighth.

These were days of rejoicing, but the booming of cannon, the huzzas and the music only drowned the sounds of weeping for dear ones who had gone away with the company, but whose places were vacant now, who slept on Southern battlefields or had died in foul prison pens. Many in the ranks were but shadows of their former selves, some had been left behind in the hospitals and others had come home to die. The first duty of the Light Guard was to bring home the dead. The bodies of Samuel W. Joyce, George Henry Champlin and George H. Lewis were sent home through the personal supervision of Captain Hutchins, who was called South to testify in the trial of the commander of Salisbury Prison.

Originally published in vol. 5, 1902.

The Dedication of the Soldiers' Monument
Helen Tilden Wild

Although Usher's *History of Medford* contains a picture of the monument erected in honor of those citizens of Medford who fell in their country's defense, there is no record given of the ceremony of dedication. Pamphlets containing the oration and flimsy four-page programs are the only records of the services, and probably only a few of these exist. The date of the consecration was September 6, 1866. A procession formed in the square at one o'clock in the afternoon.

Mr. Brooks's address was published later by the Lawrence Light Guard, and dedicated to it. Many of his utterances seem strained, now that the stress of those terrible years is passed, but we cull the following extracts, which contain words worth consideration today.

Civil War veterans from the Medford Grand Army of the Republic post, at Oak Grove Cemetery, Memorial Day, 1888.

Soldiers, neighbors, and fellow-citizens,

You all know why we have come to this city of the dead. Upon the sides of this solid and beautiful cenotaph are graven, in letters of stone, the following names:

Lieut. Col. J.G. Chambers, Lieut. William H. Burbank, Edward Gustine, L.M. Fletcher, Frank A. Keen, E. Sprague, D.T. Newcomb, D. Nolan, A.H. Stacy, D. McGillicuddy, S. Harding, J. Stetson, J.M. Powers, C.W. Willis, F. Curtin, James Haley, J.P. Hubbell, James Bierne, A. Joyce, Patrick Gleason, Augustus Tufts, R. Livingston, F.J. Curtis, B.J. Ellis, H.G. Currell, E. Ireland, William H. Rogers, William Harding, H.R. Hathaway, H. Mills, G.H. Lewis, J.M. Garrett, D.S. Cheney, R.W. Cheslyn, M. O'Connell, Sergt. S.M. Stevens, Sergt. J.T. Morrison, J.M. Fletcher, E.B. Hatch, R.C. Hathaway, G.H. Champlin, C.H. Coolidge, S.W. Joyce.

The front side, in raised letters, reads thus: "In honor of the Medford Volunteers who sacrificed their lives in defence of the Union. Fallen heroes leave fragrant memories. 1866." Forty-three self-sacrificing patriots. Twelve of our brothers were killed in battle; twelve died in prison; three died of their wounds; and the rest died of disease.

This beautiful color, waving the stripes and stars before you, was torn in three places by rifle-balls. It was presented by the ladies of Medford to the Lawrence Light Guard, and carried by them to the front in Virginia; and, when they were called into battle, William H. Lawrence, with a firm and dauntless step, carried it forward, facing the foe, and calling to his comrades to hasten after him; and, at the moment when he was ordered to retreat, a ball pierced his heart, and he fell dead upon his flag, where his blood can now be seen in its folds. It is another precious memorial among us of bravery and of death.

Medford honors itself in honoring its martyrs; and, as long as this granite column endures, succeeding generations will read it with gratitude. It is a most fit expression of our thankful hearts to those young lovers of their country, who were ready to leave father and mother, wife and children, and expose their lives to the shot and bayonets of a host of infuriated rebels. Their burning thought was to save their country. They died, but their country lives. Let there be no bounds, then, to our gratitude; and, as long as memory lives, let the names on this monument be sanctified in our hearts; and let it be used, moreover, to express our gratitude to all the skilful officers and brave men of the army and navy who achieved such decisive victories over the enemies of our country.

This memorial shaft speaks to us also of our manhood and national character. The rush of our heroes to the ranks, when they heard the first *gun against Fort Sumter, proved—what? It proved, conclusively, that we had a New England, and a national character already formed in the souls of these patriots, lying silent and unseen till the country called for it; and, when it did call, it found these men to be intense Americans, intense New Englanders, intense Medfordites. Medford recognized them with one universal shout of approbation.*

Have not these facts taught us about our manhood and our national character? We feel now, as this generation has never felt before, the vital force of patriotic principle, and the solemn obligation of patriotic duty. Do we not feel this new meaning of the word patriotism tingling from our central heart to every extremity? Our soldiers and sailors have taught us this, and are they not our permanent benefactors? They have brought to light this new nation in our midst.

Again, these memorial pillars testify to the power of our Constitution to bear the new and untried strain of a gigantic civil war. Our Constitution proved a safe compass on a stormy sea.

Furthermore, this column suggests to us our duties. It asks us to love our Union more and more every month, and to watch with eagle eyes the doings of its enemies.

Among the imperative and Christian duties of our country now is the education of the freedmen. In the immortal proclamation of President Lincoln, January 1, 1863, there is an implied promise that the United States would instruct the freedmen in the new rights and new duties of their new condition. That divine proclamation changed all the slaves—into what? Not into orangoutangs, not into angels, but into citizens. Citizens they are, nothing more and nothing less; and, as citizens and human beings, they have as much right to instruction and development as they have right to food. At this moment, they ask of us this bread: shall we give them a stone?

This granite pillar seems to connect itself with all the parts and questions of our civil war. It calls up the marvellous ingenuity of our people, shown from the iron-clads and cannon to defend our cities, and destroy our enemies, to the Sanitary Commission to heal our wounded, and feed our hungry; from man in his noble daring, to woman in her angel ministries.

Soldiers and fellow-citizens, we now solemnly bequeath this hallowed monument to our succeeding generations in Medford. Let it stand in its simple power, protected, not only from sacrilegious hands, but from thoughtless fracture, misplaced pencillings, and offensive scratches. Let nothing be done to it that can lessen its silent eloquence, or destroy its patriotic design.

Glimpses of Medford: Selections from the *Historical Register*

We have given it in our hearts to our successors. When your children's children shall read the history of our dreadful war, and understand its momentous tendencies, then will they come to this consecrated monument, blackened as it will be by the storms of a century, and read with swelling hearts the names of the Medford volunteers who sacrificed their lives in defence of the Union. Fifty years hence, let the hoary-headed soldier come, and kneel in prayer as he calls to mind the young friend who fell at his side. Here let the aged mother come to read the name of her patriot son. Here let the statesman come to learn what union and liberty have cost. Here let the historian come to meditate on those central truths which shape the destinies of the world. Here let the poet come, and celebrate in sweetest lays the victories of truth and the triumph of right. Here let love come, that it may carry away inspiration; and beauty come, that she may leave here her garlands.

Originally published in vol. 9, 1906.

Chapter 5

TURNPIKES, TAVERNS AND OTHER INDUSTRIES

MEDFORD TURNPIKE CORPORATION
John H. Hooper

On March 2, 1803, the General Court of the Commonwealth of Massachusetts, upon the petition of Benjamin Hall, John Brooks, Fitch Hall, Ebenezer Hall II and Samuel Buel, granted to these petitioners the right to lay out and make a turnpike road from the easterly side of the road nearly opposite to Dr. Luther Stearns's house, and running easterly of Winter Hill and Plowed Hill to the east side of the road opposite Page's tavern near the neck in Charlestown.

The act provided that the corporation shall be entitled to receive from each traveler or passenger the following rate of toll, to wit: for every coach, chariot, phaeton or other four-wheeled carriage for the conveyance of persons, drawn by not more than two horses, ten cents, and if drawn by more than two horses an additional sum of two cents for each horse; for every cart, wagon, sleigh or sled or other carriage of burden, drawn by not more than three cattle, six cents, if by more than three, an additional sum of two cents for every additional ox or horse.

January 26, 1804, a committee was chosen to consider the expediency of building a hotel. At a subsequent meeting the committee reported that it was inexpedient to build at present. No action by the corporation concerning the building of a hotel was taken after the appointment of this committee, as the building of the Medford House commencing about this time obviated the necessity of any further action. February 13, 1804, the standing committee was directed to purchase a piece of land on or near the farm of General Derby and build a house suitable for a toll man. The committee contracted with Buckman and Wait, carpenters, to build the house at a cost of $300. Mr. James Kidder was appointed toll-gatherer, his compensation for the year following to be $350 and the use of the house.

The foregoing history of the Medford Turnpike Corporation is taken largely from the record book of the corporation. It is evident that the undertaking was not a profitable one, and that during the last thirty years of its existence it was the main object of the proprietors to rid themselves of the burden of its maintenance.

The turnpike road was used by the sporting portion of the community as a course for the speeding of horses. There was a tree that stood on the southerly side of the road that was just one mile from the old saw and gristmill. The only disadvantages experienced by the sportsmen were the clouds of dust that filled the air, for the road was about the dustiest place to be found far or near.

We never heard of the toll-gatherer being robbed of a busy day's receipts, as was the case in other places, but the turnpike road was once the scene of a sensational highway robbery, when Major Bray was held up and robbed by the notorious highwayman Mike Martin. It is said that on Mrs. Bray's handing over her watch, the "knight of the road" immediately returned it, saying he "never robbed a lady."

The old tollhouse on the Medford turnpike.

It was quite a common sight to see Colonel Samuel Jaques of the Ten-hills Farm, bugle in hand, ride up and down the road to and from the hunting grounds mounted on his hunting horse and followed by a pack of hounds.

Originally published in vol. 23, 1920.

THE FOUNTAIN TAVERN
John H. Hooper

Under the date of April 29, 1702, Mr. Peter Seccomb of Medford bought of Mr. John Bradstreet two and one half acres of land bounded northeast and east on the road into Charlestown woodlots; southerly on the road from Malden to Charlestown; westerly upon said Bradstreet's other land. Three years later, July 4, 1705, Mr. Bradstreet sold to Mr. Seccomb an additional lot containing one half an acre. These two lots composed the Fountain House estate. The house must have been built soon after these purchases, for in the year 1713, Mr. Seccomb was licensed as an inn holder, and no doubt was the first landlord of the Fountain Tavern. In December of that year he sold his estate to Messrs. Francis Leath and son, and the place for the first time was called the Fountain Tavern. Mr. Leath Sr. was landlord in the year 1714.

A romantic view of the Fountain Tavern on Salem Street.

During that year the estate was deeded back to Mr. Seccomb, who immediately sold to Captain Samuel Wade. In the year 1715, and for many years after, Captain Wade was landlord of this tavern. In the year 1735 he sold the estate to Messrs. Stephen Hall Jr., Stephen and Simon Bradshaw. In the year 1751, Mr. Simon Bradshaw sold one half of a house to Mr. Stephen Bradshaw, and it was described as "at a place formerly called the Fountain."

By this sale Mr. Stephen Bradshaw came into possession of the whole estate. Mr. Bradshaw sold it in the year 1765 to Mr. Jonathan Patten. In the year 1775 Mr. Thomas Bradshaw was listed as an inn holder, and from that year until the year 1789, he kept the Fountain Tavern. In the year 1795 Mr. Patten's widow sold to Mr. Nathaniel Hall. From Mr. Hall the estate passed through the ownership of many different persons down to the present day. There is no evidence that this house was used as a tavern from the year 1734 until the year 1775, when it was occupied by Mr. Bradshaw. Although it is very probable that it was sometimes used as a place where liquors were sold, it is not likely that it was used as a tavern after Mr. Bradshaw's day. The late Mr. Rufus Sawyer took down the old building and erected on its site the house now standing on the easterly corner of Salem and Fountain Streets.

Originally published in vol. 8, 1905.

LOOKING BACKWARD
Eliza M. Gill

My father, Solomon Manning, was born in Chelmsford, Massachusetts, in 1799. His mother was Lucy Andrews of Carlisle. Father was in the employ of Mr. Dudley Hall of Medford from 1820 to 1825. Mr. Hall owned a large amount of land extending north into what is now known as the Fells. Considerable domestic stock was kept, and butter and cheese were made on the farm. The stock barns were north of the Hall homestead on the hill. To get to them there were fifty stone steps up the steep ascent just back of the house. The granite steps were taken from Tyngsboro, coming by boats on the Middlesex Canal.

Farming was done with oxen. Mr. Hall also had a distillery where Medford rum was made. Molasses was brought from the wharves in Boston to Medford by ox teams and boats called Gundelows. My father did the teaming, and has told me he had many times arrived in Boston, five miles away, with a load of rum by sunrise when the thermometer was below zero. There was no complaint of hard work or long days then. One day Mr. Hall said to father, who was his foreman or outside manager, "Solomon, I hope you will not drink this rum we make here, it is damaging to drink it. It is ruining many young men who came down from the country, as you did." The rum jug was carried along with hired men (then all Americans) and was considered very necessary when haying on the marsh.

I can remember well as far back as 1830 when but few farmers thought it proper to get through the haying season without from ten to forty gallons of rum and the stores in my part of New Hampshire sold from fifty to one hundred hogsheads of new rum a year. It was sent usually by ox and horse teams, 20 to 150 miles back into the country. I remember the six- and eight-horse teams toiling over the dirt and sandy roads and mud and snow in their season; also the nine-stage coaches that ran through Bedford, past our house from Concord to Nashua up to the time the cars reached Concord in June 1842. After that we saw no more stagecoaches. Few farmers required rum after the Washingtonian Revolution in 1840. The pledge then so freely taken was something like this: "So here we pledge perpetual hate, To all that can intoxicate."

A view of the distillery area on Riverside Avenue. The distillery is the second building on the right, Richard Sprague House on the corner.

The foregoing account was written for me by Jacob W. Manning of Reading, the well-known nurseryman, a few years before his death, as being possibly of some interest to Medford people. Mr. Manning was born in Bedford, New Hampshire, February 20, 1826, and died in Reading, Massachusetts, September 16, 1904. The account is just as it came from the veteran's hand.

Originally published in vol. 15, 1912.

THE CUTTER FAMILY AND ITS CONNECTION WITH A TIDE MILL IN MEDFORD
William R. Cutter

John Cutter (of the fifth generation from Richard Cutter), who was son of Gershom and Anna (Fillebrown) Cutter, owned (probably hired) a tide mill in Medford, afterward occupied by his son Gershom Cutter. He was born in Menotomy, in that part of Cambridge now known as Arlington, Massachusetts, September 26, 1737, and died in Medford, where he long pursued the occupation of a miller, on October 16, 1788.

Tide mill where the Mystic River meets the lower Mystic Lake on the Arlington side.

The son John, of the above-named John, born at Menotomy, July 26, 1770, married Mary, daughter of Stephen and Mary (Hill) Hall, of Medford. This man, known as Captain John Cutter from his connection with the militia of Medford, died in Woburn, in that part known as Winchester, Massachusetts, November 23, 1825. His wife, who was born June 22, 1772, died February 27, 1848. He assumed the charge of his father's tide or gristmill when his father died. His mother continued to occupy the old mill house for some two or three years after her husband's death, and then John married and dwelt there himself. He had quite a career as a miller in the West Indies and Canada, and really was quite an enterprising man. Not long after 1801 he built a windmill in Medford for grinding grain. At Medford also he became one of the earliest fishermen on an extensive scale in the Mystic River. For this right, in 1803, he paid sixty-five dollars, the privilege being more particularly near the "Dike" or "Labor in Vain," and he often piloted vessels at this time between Medford and Boston. He owned lighters and transported brick to the city, some of which are now seen in the buildings on Central Wharf and Doctor Sharp's (now Charles Street) church. In 1810, having purchased the gristmill of Caleb Richardson in Woburn, latterly known as the Cutter's mill, in Cutter's village, in Winchester, he built a new structure with two run of stone, which he improved and occupied until his death. In 1817 he built a gristmill in North Chelsea run by tide water, which was occupied by his sons until the year 1830, when they sold the estate and removed to Winchester.

Zachariah Cutter, a brother of the last-named John, carried on the old tide mill in Medford for a number of years, and then went to Milton, Massachusetts, and engaged in the same business. His death occurred in 1808.

The title to the Cutter tide mill in Medford appears to be as follows, according to the published history of Medford: In 1746 the tide mill near Sandy Bank was built, the first of its kind in that part of the town. Its origin arose in articles of agreement between a number of citizens, owners of the land and a number of other citizens who were the undertakers of the enterprise. These articles were dated February 20, 1746. Certain procedure was necessary to complete the undertaking, such as giving lands, opening a straight road from the market to the mill site and building a stone bridge over Gravelly Creek for the mill's accommodation, the building of a dam, etc. The mill was to be ready for use before the last day of September 1746. It was successfully completed and answered well its purpose. Timothy Waite Jr. acquired possession at an early period in its history. Seth Blodget bought it of him on March 9, 1761. Matthew Bridge followed Blodget on October 18, 1780. Mr. Bridge disposed of it to the Bishops—John Sr. and John Jr.—

in 1783 and 1784, and John Bishop, probably the junior, sold the whole to Gershom Cutter, who was followed in ownership by Samuel Cutter, George T. Goodwin and Joseph Manning.

Originally published in vol. 3, 1900.

MEDFORD BRANCH RAILROAD

The facts are, the Medford Branch Railroad Company had but a brief existence, while the Branch Railroad has been in public service over seventy years. The original incorporators (as they were privileged by the charter to do) disposed of their charter and franchise to the Boston & Maine. We have before us a printed copy of the latter's petition to the county commissioners of Middlesex, which sets forth that fact, and also that it had undertaken to construct the "Branch," had filed location thereof according to law and was desirous to proceed with construction forthwith. Then follow the names of the property owners along the line with whom question of land damage was unsettled, beginning with Luther Angier at Main Street and ending with William Bradbury at the other end. The petition was signed by the president of the Boston & Maine, Thomas West.

A stylish reproduction of the first train to come through Medford in 1837. The train and its occupants were part of the tercentenary celebration in 1930.

On the first Tuesday in June 1846, at their meeting at Concord, the commissioners ordered the petitioners to give notice to all these interested persons and corporations of its meeting for a view, and a hearing at the Medford Hotel on "10th of August next, at ten of the clock in the forenoon, by serving each of the land owners named with a copy of this petition and order thereon, fourteen days before said view," etc. The copy mentioned is endorsed as to Mrs. Eliza Perkins and is attested by the signature of "John T. White, Constable of Medford." In all there were forty or more. The only corporation we notice is the First Baptist Society in Malden.

We must accept this as "documentary evidence" that the Medford Branch Railroad Company had but brief existence, and that the Branch Railroad was built by the Boston & Maine and always has been a part of its system. And now arises the query, just when was it built and when did it begin operation of passenger service? In the reports of railroads to the state, that of 1846, the Boston & Maine reports "9 65/1000 miles of branch road of single track." Of this the Medford Branch is a little less than two miles (9,800 feet) according to Hayward's survey, and is probably included in this report. We base this conclusion upon the statements of the foregoing petition and the date of commissioners' view of location, as compared with the time of running the first trains. Who knows when that "eleven-ton engine, built at Lowell," with two cars first traversed the branch? Inquiry among the oldest residents of Medford has so far been unavailing. The "documentary evidence" available is this: up to and including March 1, 1847, the Boston & Maine Railroad advertisement in the *Boston Advertiser* announces no train service to Medford.

In the issue of March 2 appears,

> *Medford to Boston 6½ & 8 A.M. 1¾ & 5½ P.M.*
> *Boston to Medford 7¼ & 9 A.M. 2½ & 5:50 P.M.*

The above we consider as conclusive evidence that the Medford Branch began operation on that day, and was obtained from the file of the *Boston Advertiser*. We found no mention of it in the news columns, though we did notice that on the Fitchburg Railroad at Cambridge, on the previous day, the snow ploughs were derailed and engines sent out from Boston to clear the track—a sidelight on the weather conditions of the time.

Of the cost of building the Medford Branch, and whether it tallied with Mr. Hayward's estimate, we have no means of knowing. The reports to the state are complete and answer the law's requirements, but are for the entire system, and other than tabulated matter are very brief and deal mainly with the accidents that occurred.

We have seen in print the statement that its cost was $38,208.60. At this point comes a matter of interest that is now forgotten. It was proposed to build the road on the south side of the river, and just here is a lesson in local geography with a touch of local history also, with a little of engineering thrown in. Fifty years before, this last had been shown in the survey and construction of the Middlesex Canal along the Mystic marshes of Charlestown and Medford, but for the last ten of the fifty the competition of the Boston and Lowell Railroad had been disastrous to the waterway. The charter of the latter railroad allowed no other railroad into Lowell for forty years, but there was no hindrance toward Boston. The canal embankments could be used as a roadbed for the Medford Branch, and the cut through the ledgy shoulder of Winter Hill in the corner of Medford and Charlestown was already made. The canal was but little used, and a proposition to discontinue it as a waterway, and by the laying of iron pipes along the ten miles of the southern end to Woburn utilize it as a water supply for Boston, had just been made. Mr. Hayward said:

To the expense of building the branch, I have added that of building a second track on the Maine Extension Road, from the proposed junction with that road to the Middlesex canal, where the route proposed on the south side of the river would meet the Extension road. This I do, that we may have all the data for comparing the two routes proposed.

This expense (in five items) amounted to $9,652.60, and, added to the estimate already given, total $34,735.10, to which 10 percent ($3,473.50) was added for engineer, contingencies, etc., making $38,208.60. As yet we have not ascertained the actual cost of the branch, as only the accounts of the Boston & Maine can give proof.

By this it appears that the recent "Interurban" project and even the defunct Mystic Valley were not the first to consider a way paralleling the Medford turnpike. Mr. Hayward placed his report before "Messrs. Bishop, Lawrence and others," the incorporators of the railroad (Mr. Usher says a committee of citizens employed him), closing thus: "The distance to Boston by the northern route is thirty-two hundred feet greater than that by the southern route; and the southern branch will be forty-two hundred feet longer than the northern." They decided for the shorter branch, all within the bounds of Medford, but the longer distance to Boston.

It was twenty years before the Wellington district began to increase materially in growth. To be sure, some ten years later, Editor Moody of the original Medford journal suggested "a suspension bridge to the highlands of Somerville," but he was ahead of the times. Not until Middlesex Avenue was opened, with its bridge across the Mystic, had that peninsular district a direct outlet to Boston, and even then its growth was slow.

Above: Mystic River at the Boston Avenue Bridge in 1899 at the point where the Middlesex Canal crossed the river. The bridge was built on the original abutments.

Opposite: Bridge that formerly went over the Middlesex Canal. This last vestige of the canal was photographed on the Brooks Estate in West Medford, circa 1880.

GLIMPSES OF MEDFORD: SELECTIONS FROM THE HISTORICAL REGISTER

In the second year of service, 1848, there were three accidents reported:

April 28 James Gregg, having laid down between the rails on a curve near Medford, was run over by an engine and killed instantly.

May 5 Samuel Baldwin, in getting out of the cars at Medford after they had started, was struck by the baggage car and his arm was broken.

November 4 James Pratt, Medford, legs broken by collision at Medford Junction.

In 1853 Enos Ormsbee and Silas Bumpus of Charlestown, carpenters, walking on the track to Medford, were instantly killed by the 7¾ A.M. northern train, the So. Reading train passing at the same time. [This must have been below the Junction and not on the Branch.]

And another in which the Medford Branch figures: "June 28, 1854, L.G. Brown killed at Causeway street [Boston]. He was driving with two others when his horse became unmanageable and dashed open the gate. Brown was struck by outward Medford train." Doubtless there are those who remember that for some years locomotives were not allowed to cross Causeway and Traverse Streets in Boston, and that the trains were hauled by horses to the locomotives waiting just below Causeway Street and also inwardly.

Another report throws a little light on the manner of operating the Branch: "January 3, 1854, Saugus and Medford train coming in at 2.20 P.M., Baggage Master Caleb Eames, Jr., of Saugus, killed near freight house owing to misplaced switch." This record indicates that some Medford Branch trains were attached to other inward trains at Medford Junction and the combined train taken over the main line to Boston by one engine. A similar arrangement was obtained on other roads. Such would have left the Medford engine free to return with cars brought to the Junction by another outward train, and better accommodated the time schedule.

This Branch Railroad certainly was of great service to Medford in its earlier years, and had its first competitor in passenger service in the Medford and Charlestown Horse Railroad in 1860. This continued until 1873, but it is questionable if the long haul over Winter Hill was very attractive to Medford people, other than the few who dwelt along its line, and even its operation attracted few new residents. This road was taken over by the Middlesex Corporation and in 1873, after eleven years, discontinued. Reopened in 1884, it extended to West Medford and Malden, and soon after operated by electricity, it became a powerful competitor. Taking its patrons at their very doors and landing them at their places of business is an advantage the steam railway with its fixed terminals cannot offer, even were it electrified. So the problem remains.

"Honest Mike" Griffin, railroad guard at the High Street crossing in West Medford from 1878 to 1906.

An early Boston & Maine Railroad train.

Of the engineer's estimate for depot buildings, the larger part went into the terminal station on Main Street. Printed views show it in its various appearances to date, and incidentally some other changes near the square.

Near the other end of the Branch one resident still remains who witnessed the building and opening of the branch—the oldest man in Medford, J. Everett Wellington. His name does not appear in the petition referred to, as his family gave the strip of land the railroad required. It crossed their orchard, and he tells us that on the Fourth of July, 1846, "we dug up and replanted ten sizable apple trees. Apples were already formed on them, but all the trees lived and bore fruit that year." Of the many trees in that orchard, over which numerous houses have been built, a few still remain, but have suffered for want of care in these later years. One of the conditions of land grant was that all Medford Branch trains should stop there. At first there was no station house, a signal was shown. After a while a little "shack" was provided for shelter, and later a station house erected.

We had a pleasant interview with Wellington recently, sitting on the lawn and looking over the village grown up around his home. A whole history might and should be written of this corner of Medford called by his name and practically bounded landward by the Medford Branch Railroad.

Originally published in vol. 20, 1917.

WITHINGTON BAKERY
Moses Whitcher Mann

During the first week in May the old buildings so long the home of the Medford cracker and baking industry were demolished. The vine-clad dwelling with its lattice entrance and the quaint old gambrel-roofed store and its shed containing all the ovens are all gone. The place is the scene of busy activity in the erection of the theatre that is to cater to the amusement-seeking public.

There have been three Henry Withingtons. The first appears on the tax list in 1799, and lived in the old brick building called the "College," which faced the river on "the way to Blanchard's," afterward called Ship Street. There the second Henry was born on August 9, 1800, just prior to the beginning of shipbuilding by Thatcher Magoun. The old mill beside the river, and the lighters and molasses-laden vessels to the distillery, had his boyish attention, and perhaps he may have assisted his father at the tollgate on the Andover turnpike a mile from the marketplace. Evidently his youthful mind did not fix itself on his father's trade, that of a cordwainer or shoemaker, for he found employment in the household of the Honorable Timothy Bigelow. As "scullion" he styled himself, and perhaps his service in Squire Bigelow's house inclined him to what became his lifelong occupation. In recent years his successors placed on their sign "Established 1825."

Henry Withington had never learned the trade or business of baker by apprenticeship, but with good judgment gained by observation "took up" the occupation and, with a partner and employing experienced help, started in business in that year. The ovens that Withington and Lane used were those of some earlier baker and were located in the rear of Mr. Barker's house.

After two years Mr. Lane went out and Mr. Withington continued in business by himself. But on December 25, 1827, he took in another partner, as he married Eunice Blanchard, daughter of the famous Medford innkeeper, the ceremony being performed by the Reverend Caleb Stetson, who had early in that year begun a pastorate in Medford of twenty-one years. They came to live in the house on Salem Street, across River Street from the ancient burial ground, which was over thirty years ago moved next the common.

In 1830 Mr. Withington moved into the old house now demolished, leasing it for five years. He transferred the baking operations to the shop and ovens formerly of Convers Francis, which were in the rear of the Francis residence on a lane that has since become Ashland Street.

At the expiration of his lease he had so well established himself that he purchased the houses he occupied (and where his son Henry was born on August 30, 1832), together with the land extending backward and on which the new theatre is being built.

Up to 1840 all the bakery work was done by hand, but in 1845 he purchased machinery for making crackers. The old process was interesting. A small piece of dough was rolled under each palm, thus making two at a time. These were flattened by a rolling pin and docked, i.e., pricked by hand. This latter was done by the children. It caused the mass to split in the middle; otherwise it would rise like a biscuit. The steam generated in the baking dough passed out through the holes, and left the mass adhering to the edge and easily separated or cracked—hence the name crackers. Mr. Withington did not originate the Medford cracker. That was done by Convers Francis, who in 1797 succeeded his former master, Ebenezer Hall, in business in Medford, and continued there some twenty years until he retired.

The Medford invention of Mr. Francis seems not to have suffered in any wise under the Withington manufacture, and its fame became more extended and his product an article of export. A Medford traveler found "Medford Crackers" in the shops of London in 1834.

Withington Bakery on Salem Street. The bakery was in business continuously from 1825 to 1915.

In 1862, the third Henry Withington succeeded to the business. He also "took it up," his father assisting, and enlarged the same, adding other machinery and removing one of the earlier ovens. In place of this he erected a rotary oven and introduced a steam engine, supplanting the horsepower of previous years.

Besides crackers the elder Withington made the standard brick loaf, the two-cent roll, cakes with sugar, molasses gingerbread, seedcakes and buns. The younger added oyster, oatmeal, graham and soda biscuit to the cracker list, as well as various kinds of pies.

To keep the output of the bakery ready on time, there was a night and day force of workmen. Each Sunday, 650 loaves were sold. The writer remembers walking from his home a mile and a half away in his first year of housekeeping in 1870—a half-loaf sufficed for two—and wrapped in that old-time brown paper it kept his hands warm on the homeward journey; and it tasted good too. The usual amount made was 500 to 1,000 loaves for bread daily, reaching 1,400 at one time.

Mr. Withington sold out to Ewen McPherson in 1885, and he later to Mr. Barker, who some years ago gave up the business, since which time little or nothing has been done there, the last occupants of the shop being the Order of Moose, whatever that may be.

Mr. Henry Withington III still lives but a few rods away, is hale and hearty and for twenty-two years has faithfully served his native city as one of the board of assessors. He is still at his old post, doing as faithful, honorable work there as in the old days and old bakery, which is now only a memory.

Originally published in vol. 18, 1915.

Medford Milkmen
Francis A. Wait

In Mr. Wait's reminiscences, which follow, there is ample opportunity to read between the lines by comparison with present-day methods, remembering that the first railroad train passed through Medford only ten years before his "driving milk wagon," and that the men he mentions relied mostly on their Boston customers' patronage. From it may be formed some idea of the strenuous life of a hardy set of men of two generations past.

When Medford was a farming town, as in the old time, ere the rise of shipbuilding, more butter and cheese was made and less milk sold. With its increased population and the growing city of Boston there came a market for milk, and the business increased accordingly. The wagon business felt its influence also, and Medford-built milk wagons were in demand because of their excellent and thorough workmanship.

Mr. Francis Wait, now over fourscore years, tells much of interest and of his own experience in the business over sixty-five years ago.

Mr. Joseph E. Ober, the veteran grocer of West Medford, was formerly in the milk business and tells of his route, which he bought of one Hadley, who conducted it before the Civil War. Mr. Ober lived at the "Foot of the Rocks" in Arlington but kept no cows, receiving his milk from farmers in Lexington and Billerica and supplying customers in Medford each day with the product of the previous day's milking. Seventy-five cans of eight quarts each was the usual quantity he delivered. The milkmen usually wore long blue frocks and jumped from the wagon steps with a big can in one hand and a tin quart measure in the other, leaving the horse, who had learned the route, to stop at his own sweet will, which depended somewhat upon the proximity of the next customer's house. In cold weather that quart measure varied a little as the mercury lowered toward zero, doubtless adding to the milkman's profits, and some canny housewives were known to kindly furnish some boiling water before receiving their daily supply, thriftily saving the mixture obtained for the family pig, perhaps. Beside the kitchen door was the printed "milk score," with blank spaces numbered up to thirty-one, in which the milkman marked any "extra milk" supplied. Among Mr. Ober's customers was the famous Mystic Hall Seminary, though it had a few cows of its own. The price at that time was five cents per quart, but during the war it rose to twelve cents. No inconsiderable number of householders kept cows of their own and supplied a neighbor or two with milk.

The writer recalls his own experience, in the early morning of his first day of housekeeping, of going to a neighbor a quarter-mile away (West Medford was thinly settled then), pitcher in hand, ere breakfast for two was served. The four cents paid for that pint of milk was the first item (after the parson's fee) of his household expense. Before evening a regular supply was engaged from another neighbor who had, besides a cow, several boys who distributed the surplus of milk on their way to school.

After a few years we, too, found a cow—"a good thing to have in the family," which had increased somewhat—and also supplied some neighbors. Several others did likewise, until there came to be too much quarrel over the free pasturage we depended on, and we reluctantly parted with old Brindle and called in the regular milkman again. This was in 1880, when more than a dozen cows might have been seen tethered by a long rope or chain on the vacant land between Boston Avenue and the river. Our own experience was, doubtless, like that of others, and as more houses were built the family cow (and pig as well) was crowded out.

One of Medford's many photogenic dairy cows poses for a photographer in West Medford, circa 1880.

Now nobody sees the quart measures of those days. After a time the practice of leaving each customer's supply in a small can came in vogue, and this was superseded by the glass bottles, with dealer's name and of duly prescribed size, all according to law.

The Mr. Hadley who preceded J.E. Ober may have succeeded Mr. Milliken. Mr. Ober sold out to Lockhart & Munsey; and there was T.H. Nourse, who also came from the "Foot of the Rocks"; also a Mr. Hobbs. These were the advance guard of the present army of local milkmen.

Originally published in vol. 14, 1911.

SOME OLD MEDFORD FISH STORIES
Caleb Swan

Old Mr. Isaac Greenleaf of Medford whose house was where Mr Magoun now lives [1856] is said to have taken a peck of Tom-Cod about 1800— that were frozen stiff and hard, and put them in an upper loft, to eat them as they were wanted.

The Mystic River from the Jerome Street Bridge looking toward Arlington. The sticks in the distance are fish weirs. A fish house can be seen on the right bank.

> *After a week or two a general thaw came, and on going to get some of the fish for dinner, they were flapping and moving on the floor at a great rate.*
> *This account was common tradition in Medford and generally believed.*

Just after the history was published, Mr. Swan inserted in his copy the following item he had made note of fourteen years before:

New York, May 12, 1842.
Mr. Joseph Swan of Medford (now here) says that Mr. Russell of Medford took this month, from the Creek between the upper shipyard and Wears Bridge 107,000 alewives at one haul of the net.

As the upper shipyard of that time was located near the site of the present Winthrop Bridge, and as Mr. Swan always termed a tributary stream as far as the tide raised it a creek, the one he referred to was, doubtless, the Menotomy River. This is the largest tributary of the Mystic, has but a slight descent and is very serpentine in course. It has for a half-century been commonly known as Alewife Brook. It is highly probable that its present prosaic and diminutive name superceded the former more historic and sonorous one because of the big haul of alewives made by this Medford fisherman.

It would seem that with the improvements now being made there, it would be well to restore to it its ancient and rightful name.

Originally published in vol. 12, 1909.

MEDFORD MINING MATTERS

We naturally turn to the files of the press for information of this mining operation of 1881. The *Medford Mercury*, then in its first year of publication, under date of September 17, tells of a visit made by reporters of four Boston dailies. The occasion was enlivened by the presence of ladies, and somebody's "Old Bill" furnished the motive power up Forest Street to the Spot Pond House. From thence the party walked through the woods to the scene of operations. There the writer, who signs himself S.W.G., had "a half-hour interview with Mr. Harrigan," from which he deduced the following:

> *This mine was discovered by F.W. Morandi of Malden, who was wandering through the Fells for pleasure. He immediately purchased a large tract of land, and contracted for the sinking of a shaft 25 feet deep with a Mr. Halliday. The shaft is now 12 feet deep, the workmen having been about two weeks at work, putting in from 3 to 5 blasts per day, each bringing forth encouraging results. Mr. Harrigan told us, that if in going down the next ten feet the richness increased as it had thus far, the mine would be a paying investment, and in all probability the shaft would be sunk 100 feet.*
>
> *The first assay yielded $18 in silver, $4 in gold, and the estimate is at present $50 per ton, with copper in large proportions both in sulphide and oxide. The ore is taken to the smelting works in East Boston. About a mile northeast, Matthew Roberton has discovered silver, which is supposed to be an outcropping from the same vein.*

On October 15 appears:

> *That silver mine at Spot Pond is progressing favorably. The shaft has been sunk to a depth of 30 feet, and Mr. Harrigan has contracted to carry it 25 feet farther down. It is understood that the yield is satisfactory thus far, and that more land will be bought for mining purposes.*

The remains of the old silver mine in the Middlesex Fells. This photograph was taken in 1934.

The above is all that our local paper tells of the mining operations in a technical way. Thirty-three years had elapsed when we made our query. It was prompted by a telephone inquiry made by someone unknown to us—yes, we have a lot of such, as some take us for an information pagoda. We replied, "There was something of the kind, but we have no definite knowledge of it—no—no—we can't tell any lies about it. Goodbye." Some weeks later a very readable and interesting story appeared in the Sunday issue of a Boston paper, with a view of the locality. It located the mine on land of Mr. Willis, and says, "The shaft was sunk to a depth of eighty-five feet, encountering a spring that caused much trouble and that a lateral tunnel was excavated for seventy-five feet and that there all trace of silver was lost." Also that "the work was prosecuted for two years and after $10,000 was expended, ceased for lack of capital."

Who in Medford would have risked a pair of old shoes on the prophecy that in the course of the year silver mines would come to light within the bounds of the town? And yet an enterprising genius has brought to light in the vicinity of Spot Pond veritable silver mines, in which there is a stratum of bright possibilities, if nothing more. The resolute miner has faith in his mines and holds out the brightest kind of promise. We hope he will not be disappointed.

The recent writer, to whom we have alluded, tells that boys overturned the engine into the shaft, and the debris of crushed rock had filled it somewhat. To satisfy our curiosity, and equipped with the park commissioners' map, we recently repaired to the "old silver mine." We found "a hole in the ground," or rather in the ledge, rectangular in shape, about eight by ten feet, and perhaps nine in depth. We noted the mound of debris piled beside it, now overgrown, as nature has been kindly at work. We wondered if the *Mercury* man's "bright stratum of possibilitie" still remains in the lateral seventy-five-foot tunnel the other mentioned, or whether, indeed, that tunnel was purely mythical.

Originally published in vol. 19, 1916.

Chapter 6

AROUND THE TOWN IN THE 1800S

HIGH STREET ABOUT 1820
Helen Tilden Wild

About a hundred rods from Weir Bridge, on the north side of High Street, was a small house owned by Spencer Bucknam, occupied by a Mr. Peirce, afterward by Isaac Greenleaf for a few years and then torn down. Mr. Greenleaf lived afterward on Fulton Street.

On the south side of the street was the Payson farm of some fifty acres. The house and other buildings were a few rods from the Middlesex Canal. Elijah Smith and family occupied this place from 1800 to 1830. Mr. Smith was born in Lexington, Massachusetts. He was six years old when the battle of Lexington occurred, and he had a distinct remembrance of the event. The Payson farm being so near to the canal bridge, Mr. Smith's house was free and open to passengers taking the boats.

An eighth of a mile farther east lived Miss Rebecca Brooks—"Aunt Becky." Robert Caldwell lived in her house and carried on the farm. This house was remodeled and used by Mrs. T.P. Smith for a boarding school in the fifties. The school was known as Mystic Hall Seminary for Young Ladies, and was very popular in its day.

Just beyond Whitmore Brook, on the north side of the street, lived Captain Samuel Teel. This house is standing (1905) on the westerly corner of Brooks Street. A few rods east—on the easterly corner of Allston Street as now built—was a house occupied by Stephen Symmes, who afterward moved to the west side of Mystic Pond. The next occupant was Thomas Huffmaster, who was killed during the tornado of 1850. The site is now owned by the heirs of John H. Norton, whose wife was a daughter of Mr. Huffmaster.

About half a mile farther east, in the colonial mansion that still beautifies the street, resided Master Kendall, the teacher of the town school. After him came Mr. Stickney, Reverend Caleb Stetson and Jonathan Brooks, who formerly lived in the ancient dwelling still standing at the corner of Woburn Street.

"Ma'am Simonds Hill" was named in honor of Mrs. Joshua Simonds who with her daughters "Nabby" and Pamelia kept a dame school for many years in the house on the north side of High Street. It used to be sheltered from the street by large lilac bushes that grew on the slope between the sidewalk and the roadway. A face wall has been built and the sidewalk lowered, which adds to the comfort of the pedestrian and detracts from the picturesqueness of the house.

Above: A Victorian gentleman pauses to take in the view from Weir Bridge in West Medford.

Opposite: The Mystic Hall Seminary for Young Ladies on High Street. The exclusive school flourished between 1855 and 1859.

Around the Town in the 1800s

John Wade owned the house where Mr. George H. Bean, the florist, lives now. Major Wade's tannery was just east of this house, and family tradition says that he built the last named dwelling and two others opposite for his operatives.

Mr. A.D. Puffer's mansion, remodeled and moved back from the street, was the home of Major Samuel Swan and his son Joseph. This house was originally the Ebenezer Brooks mansion. Prior to 1812 the house was occupied by his half-brother, Captain Caleb Brooks, who was guardian of his nephew Ebenezer.

Jonathan Porter's house, a few years ago demolished, was the home of William Furness. This house was formerly the residence of Parson Turell. The next and nearest neighbor was "Cherry" Bucknam, so called because he made such excellent cherry rum. This house made way for Grace Church rectory. Next came the house of William Roach and, beyond, the Samuel Train House. This house was once the property of one Mr. Wyman, who preceded Mrs. Rowson as the proprietor of the famous select school for girls.

Originally published in vol. 8, 1905.

Following pages: An early photo of High Street looking east. The eighteenth-century houses of Isaac Hall and his brothers can be seen on the left-hand side.

AN OLD-TIME PICNIC
Charles Loomis

There is ever a charm in the reading of letters of earlier years, and this is especially true when the sentiments as expressed in the written words leave a pleasing impress of the writer's individuality. Such a charm, we think, attaches to a letter bearing date of Brookline, July 20, 1817, and written by Miss Fanny Searle to her sister, Mrs. Margaret Curzon, then at Havana, Cuba. In it is a description of an all-day excursion on the Middlesex Canal on July 18, 1817.

The picnic party consisted of a large gathering of who was best in the society of the old town of Boston. It was held at the "Lake of the Woods," now known as Horn Pond, in Woburn. The Indian name was Innitou. There were represented the Winthrops, Quincys, Amorys, Sullivans, Grays, Masons, Tudors, Eliots, Cabots and others. Daniel Webster and wife were also of the party. Mr. Webster was then thirty-five years of age. He had taken up his residence in Boston in August of the previous year. In the following year, 1818, he was to establish his fame at the bar by his matchless argument on the great Dartmouth College case before the Supreme Court of the United States.

But to quote from the letter:

> *Since I last wrote, many pleasant things have happened to me particularly, of these the most prominent is a day passed on the Canal, and its shores; there was such a variety in the amusements of the day, and of so choice a kind, that I felt no fatigue from 9 in the morning till 10 at night.*
>
> *We entered the boat at Charlestown at ½ past 9. The party was too large to have any stiffness; indeed there was the utmost ease and good humor without sadness through the day.*
>
> *The shores of the Canal for most of the distance are beautiful. We proceeded at the rate of 3 miles an hour, drawn by two horses, to the most romantic spot (about 9 miles from Boston) that I ever beheld.*
>
> *The lake is about twice the size of Jamaica Pond or larger, and has a small wooded island in the center. On the island was a band of musicians which began to play as soon as we landed. It seemed a scene of enchantment; Cousin Kate who was by my side seemed too much affected to speak.*
>
> *We had many wits in the party and there was no lack of bon mots. The gentlemen played off upon each other, to our amusement. When spirits flagged, we had the resource of music. Five instruments, and vocal music from Mrs Quincy, Mr Callender and occasionally Mr Webster and young May, with whom I was very much pleased, and who discovered, I thought, true modest assurance, with very good sense.*

A picnic in the Middlesex Fells in the 1870s. Spot Pond was a popular location for Victorian outings.

The ascent of the Canal was altogether new to me, and very interesting. It was all the pleasanter for having so many children to whom it was likewise a novelty—especially the locks through which we passed.

After landing, the children danced on the green under a tent or awning.

Later we enjoyed an excellent cold dinner, which we were quite hungry enough to relish. The day was the hottest of the season. After lunch, we dispersed for an hour as best pleased us.

We again re-entered the boat; tables were placed the whole length of it, on which were arranged fruit, wine, ice and glasses. It was the prevailing opinion that we had started for home too soon, so we landed at another delightful spot, where we stopped an hour.

We again entered the boat, and pursued our course a few miles, stopping near a house which we did not enter, but where coffee was served in the boat.

The children had another cotillion while the boat was descending the lock.

We walked a short distance, got into the boat again, took coffee listened to sweet strains, saw the sun descend and the moon rise, and reached our place of debarkation just after the last tints of daylight had faded.

Other parts of Miss Searle's letter are devoted to expressions of her intense enjoyment of the day as it passed and its delightful retrospection, the chatty intimacy naturally existing between sisters and her personal judgment of the various persons of the picnic party.

Originally published in vol. 22, 1919.

MEDFORD HIGH SCHOOL
Albert Smith

Medford, June 4, 1832: This institution is situated in the village of Medford, five miles from Boston. Its location is healthy and pleasant, and in every respect well suited to the purpose to which it is devoted. The pupils are under the constant supervision of their instructor, and no one is permitted to leave the premises, except in the company or with the consent of his teacher. The advantages of this system of instruction are too obvious, and have been too well tested by experience, to admit of question. The health of the pupils is carefully regarded, and while they are required to apply themselves closely during the hours of study, sufficient time is allowed for exercise and diversion. In the care of his pupils when out of school, the subscriber is assisted by a lady highly qualified for her station. Strict attention is paid to the manners and personal appearance of the boarders. Great importance is attached to religious instruction, and in daily attendance upon it, the members of the institution are taught to look upon Christianity, not as a matter of speculation, but as a powerful motive of conduct. The object kept in view is education, in its broadest sense—not the communication of knowledge merely, but likewise the formation of correct religious, mental and personal habits. The course of study in the institution comprises the following branches.

1. Ancient and modern languages.
2. Arithmetic, mental and practical; algebra and geometry.
3. Philosophy, material, intellectual and moral; the former including mechanics, astronomy, chemistry, botany and the various branches of natural science.
4. Penmanship.
5. Elocution—by which is intended the spelling and defining of words, and an accurate and judicious manner of reading poetry and prose, together with declamation.

The Medford High School on High Street. The school was built in 1843, and was enlarged several times as the town population grew.

6. Geography, history and chronology.

7. Grammar, logic and rhetoric, by textbooks and the practice of composition.

Terms—For board, washing, fuel, lights and tuition, forty dollars per quarter. Tuition of those who do not board at the Institution, six dollars per quarter. In addition for ancient languages, three dollars; for modern languages, three dollars; for the higher branches of mathematics, three dollars.

There is a female department under the care of Miss Brigham, which is so far connected with the institution as that the recitations in the languages and mathematics are heard by the principal. The course of study is similar to that described above, and the terms the same as those before specified for day scholars. Instruction is given in music, painting and drawing, to those who desire it.

The school year consists of three terms, one of sixteen and two of fifteen weeks each. The fall term will commence on Wednesday, the fifth of September.

Originally published in vol. 9, 1906.

The old town hall decorated for Independence Day, July 4, 1886.

MEDFORD SQUARE, 1835–1850
These reminiscences contributed by men and women born and bred within sight of the "Town House"

The present city hall has been built about threescore and ten years. In 1839 an addition was made on the south end. The hall floor had about four rows of slips or pews with high backs, and rising one above the other, leaving about one-third of the floor open in the center. The desk was at the south end and a gallery was opposite it, over the entrance. There were two rooms

136

on the north side on the second floor; one of them occupied by George Hervey, tailor, as a workroom. The selectmen's room was in the lower northwest corner. Mr. Hervey's tailor shop was in the northeast corner. Jonas Coburn's dry goods store occupied a large room having two entrances on Main Street. Oliver Blake's dry goods store and Mr. Randall's bookstore were in the south end of the building.

Across the square on High Street the Seccomb House was occupied by Joseph Wyman, stage driver and proprietor of a livery stable. Dr. C.V. Bemis boarded in this house when he came to Medford. His office was in the Ebenezer Hall House on Main Street, and later in the Seccomb House. H.N. Peak, William Peak and Otis Waterman were later tenants.

The next house east was owned by Joseph Patten Hall. The front was as it now stands except that there was a basement, and the first floor was approached by a long flight of steps. The back part of the house was very old and had its entrance on an alley. The outline of it can be seen on the north wall of the present building. The dwelling was occupied by Mr. Hall and his three sisters. Mr. John Howe, grocer, occupied the store on the ground floor. Later Mr. Samuel Green, who married one of the Misses Hall, occupied it for a clothing and dry goods store. He was the father of Samuel S. Green, the veteran street railway man.

The Joseph Patten Hall House in Medford Square. The grocery store was originally owned by John Howe, and later became Charles Drew's Meat and Grocery Store.

The next house easterly belonged to Turell Tufts. He was a bachelor. Miss Mary Wier was his housekeeper for years. The town is indebted to him for the shade trees on Forest Street.

On the opposite corner of Forest Street were Timothy Cotting's house and bakery. There was a driveway around the house from Forest to Salem Street. The entrance to the house was on Salem Street. The bakery, having an entrance on Forest Street, was connected with the dwelling.

Where Cotting Block stands was a low tenement house called Rotten Row. It was occupied by the families of Joseph Gleason, Timothy Brigden, Stilman Derby and the widow of Henry Withington Sr. On the site of the Mystic Church was a large house in which lived William S. Barker, grocer; the house was removed to Salem Street, opposite the common, and is now owned by heirs of S. Derby.

At the junction of Salem and Ship Streets the present brick house had for its tenants in the thirties Mr. Parsons, a ship carpenter (whose daughter married Alfred Eels); Dr. Samuel Gregg; and William Peak, who lived on Salem Street. J.V. Fletcher, butcher, occupied the northerly corner store, and Gilbert Blanchard, grocer, the southerly one.

Mr. Fletcher lived on Simond's Hill in the house now standing east of Woburn Street. His slaughterhouse was in his yard. Local butchers slaughtered their own meat at that time. Alexander Gregg, at one time a teacher in the old brick schoolhouse, lived in the Ship Street tenement, over the store. He did a large teaming business, running two large four-horse baggage wagons to and from Boston, the horses driven tandem. His stables and sheds were opposite his dwelling, extending to the river. He was a prominent man in town affairs, serving in many capacities, including representative. Between his stables and the Lawrence premises was the pottery of Thomas Sables. Some of his work is in existence today.

At the corner of Ship and Main Streets lived Mrs. Jonathan Porter. Her front door was on Main Street at the northerly end, and a side door was approached through a gate and yard from Ship Street. The rest of the building and the building adjoining were occupied by Mrs. Porter's son, George W. Porter, who was a trader, dealing in dry goods, groceries, hardware, farming tools, liquors, powder, salt, etc. Mr. Porter succeeded his father in the business. A very large willow tree projecting over the street stood directly in the sidewalk near the southerly line of the Porter property. A dock from the river that ran parallel with Main Street extended as far as Mr. Porter's premises, and probably in former years Porter's store had trade by water.

The ruins of the old Bishop distillery were on the east side of the dock. John Bishop (son of John and Mary Holmes) ran a fleet of fishing vessels that discharged and packed their cargoes on the wharf.

Next to Porter's store was Luther Angier's apothecary store. He began business in a store on the other side of the street. Mr. Angier was succeeded by Francis Kidder.

The shoe store of Mr. G.E. Dutton, 14 Main Street, has been used for that purpose for many years. Willard Butters, shoemaker, and Thomas Revallion (colored), barber, were tenants, succeeded by Oliver Blake, who later removed his dry goods store to the town house. Mr. Butters later used the abandoned tollhouse on the Andover Turnpike (Forest Street) as a shop.

Originally published in vol. 5, 1902.

THE TORNADO OF 1851

Few residents of West Medford today know or can form an idea of the scene of devastation and ruin presented in this now beautiful section of Medford after the tornado or cyclone of seventy-five years ago had passed through it.

Friday, August 22, 1851, was a hot, sultry, oppressive day. As the afternoon waned, the quiet was ominous. An old resident, who had been a sea captain, made remark, "If I was at sea I should expect a waterspout." Suddenly, at about quarter past five, there appeared in the west beyond Wear Bridge a whirling cloud, something in shape like a spreading tree or an inverted cone. Its lower part seemed to writhe about like the trunk of an elephant, reaching toward the earth. As it came on over the river, it began its terrible work as if with teeth and jaws of steel. Its track covered a space of about eighty rods wide, taking the general course of High Street with varying force and incredible velocity.

Passing over the valley of Meeting-house Brook, it continued through the woods and reappeared on Forest Street. While its general course was eastward, trees were blown in other and varying directions within the width of its track, and all sorts of freaks were later observed. A little shed or hen house escaped, while large, strongly built houses and barns were demolished. Others were unroofed, while chimney tops, windows, blinds and fences went like chaff before or with it. A freight car on the railroad siding was rolled along ten rods, then lifted from the track and landed sixty feet away, where now is Playstead Road.

Gleason's Pictorial of Boston, September 6, 1851, presented its artist's view, saying:

A scene representing the tornado at Medford, 1851.

The locality is at the east of the West Medford station. The dismantled house on the right was that occupied by Mr. Costello. The next across the road, the dwelling of Mr. Sanford, the depot master, which was moved twenty feet, crushing beneath it his son, a young man of 19 years, who was obliged to suffer amputation of both legs. The two-story house next to it was occupied by Mr. Nye, a carpenter. It was completely unroofed. In the second story Mrs. Nye and newly-born infant, injured by the wreck. In the extreme left is Captain Wyatt's house which was completely riddled.

In one house there was pasted on the wall a variety of pictures and portraits. That of then–President Fillmore was stripped off without fracture or injury and borne by the gale into a garden a half-mile away. Its finder restored it to the owner, who replaced it. Of it, Reverend Mr. Brooks remarked, "Political prophets may tell us what this foreshadows." But President Fillmore did not succeed himself in the White House.

Mrs. Caldwell (of Irving Street) took a journey on the wings of the wind and was safely set down 150 feet away. Less fortunate was one of the workmen at Mystic Street (who in 1902 visited the writer and told of his experience) on the fateful day. Living at Cambridge, he was on his way home when he was taken up and hurled into a pile of debris, from which on recovering consciousness he crawled, bruised and bleeding. A brakeman helped him into the baggage car, and procuring cotton waste from the engine stuffed it into his clothing and partially stopped his bleeding. Arriving at East Cambridge, he was taken home, where the surgeon removed a splinter five inches long, which, striking his thighbone, was deflected downward. He had never been to the village since that day to make any stop, but looked over the ground somewhat and while there met a man he knew, the late Lorin L. Dame.

One person was fatally injured, Mr. Thomas Huffmaster. Struck by a joist in the breast, he died from its effect soon after. His house was on High Street, corner of Allston, later that of his son-in-law, J.H. Norton.

The schoolhouse on Canal Street was utterly destroyed; its floor with the seats attached lay upside down across Whitmore Brook. School was to have begun the following Monday. The big Whitmore elm escaped with little injury, but a horse chestnut at Warren Street was so wrenched and twisted as to show the effect thirty years later. Another, nearby, blossomed anew in the following weeks.

The storm seemed to have begun its havoc with over $4,000 damage in Waltham, $23,606 in Arlington and $18,768 in Medford. These figures we gather from the report of a committee chosen by citizens in West Medford during the ensuing week. This report was in a neatly bound volume of seventy-two pages—forty pages by Mr. Brooks, "in the interest of science," eleven by the committee and the rest relative to West Cambridge and Waltham.

Less explicit, but terse, was the reply of one of the sufferers in relating his views: "Och! sure the wurrld has doom to an end, the houses are slivered entirely, and o'im kilt."

On Sunday following the disaster, Medford was thronged by many thousands who came to view the scene. The writer was among them, and though less than six years old then, still has vivid memories of wrecked buildings, uprooted and fallen trees and the gale at his home, five miles away. It seems miraculous that no greater loss of life occurred. Doubtless the expression made in the citizens' meeting referred to, "Now we feel ourselves called upon to acknowledge our gratitude to God for the preservation of our lives in the midst of greatest peril and danger," was heartfelt.

Originally published in vol. 29, 1926.

Stone Face in the Middlesex Fells

There are scattered here and there in this country boulders of the glacial period, some in the forests, others along the hilltops and still others storm-beaten and wave-washed by old oceans' shores, that oftentimes reveal fantastic and wonderful shapes.

Sometimes these have been all unnoticed until someone with eyes to see has come along, and then we have wondered where ours have been all the while. Such a one may be found in the Middlesex Fells at Medford.

Not far from the home of the late Elizur Wright (he who first urged the scheme of this natural park) is a woodland road leading off the old Andover Turnpike, now called Forest Street, and across Gravelly Brook. Many years ago (almost a century), a granite quarry was opened among these hills. The rock is very dark in color and much harder to work than that of Quincy or Concord. Much of it was used, however, until about fifty years ago, and the deep caverns and pits made by its removal are now seen with large trees growing in and about them.

The roadways, on which great blocks and the red gravel that was long ages ago formed of the disintegrated rock was hauled out, now make beautiful pleasure paths. The broad malls of Boston Common were dressed with this same red gravel in years past.

The snow-covered profile of the Old Man of the Fells. The rock formation was destroyed during the construction of Route 93.

Glimpses of Medford: Selections from the Historical Register

Beside one of these shaded sylvan roads may be seen the Old Man of the Fells, looking steadily and serenely across the path toward the valley of Gravelly Brook and the rocky hills beyond.

Unlike the profile of the Old Man in the Mountain at Franconia, this old man is easily accessible and is best seen close at hand, his head and shoulder risen from the ground scarce a rod away from the road. A man of ordinary stature, with outstretched hand, may barely reach the eyebrow; but this old fellow is as capricious as his north-country cousin and, like many other things in this world, your view will depend on how you look.

As you pass along over the brook, the road turns a little to the left. A shapeless mass of rock is seen among the trees, with a little sapling growing upon its top, and this is the end of an outcropping granite ledge. The quarry was opened a little farther on. As you walk slowly along a projecting rock appears at the right of the mass, and this is the old man's nose. Soon an indentation below forms the lips, and lower the chin and neck assume shape, also the retreating eyebrow and massive forehead.

If you are fortunate enough to view it just after a light snowfall, the vision is made still more realistic by the gray hair, and the Old Man of the Fells is seen in bold relief.

As you walk along, the features begin to change their expression: the nose becomes less prominent, the lips and chin disappear entirely and a few steps farther on there is nothing to be seen of the old man. There is only a confused mass of split and creviced ledge, just as some powder blast left it three generations ago, but weather-worn and blackened by the sun and storms of the years long gone.

It is doubtful if the existence of this partly natural, partly accidental sculpture is known to many people; quite likely many of those who on a pleasant summer day walk through the Fells haven't noticed him, but to the lover of nature and those who have eyes to see, the Old Man of the Fells guards this entrance thereto.

Originally published in vol. 32, 1929.

West Medford in 1870
Moses Whitcher Mann

I wish to antedate the time announced on our program, and by the president, by some years, and ask you to take a backward glimpse of the "West End," for so was that portion of Medford once called. It is not my intention to take you into ancient history, but to ask you to view the locality, first through a schoolboy's eyes. The schoolboy lived in Woburn, and the big *Lippincott's Gazetteer* on the teacher's desk informed him that his hometown was connected with Boston by the Boston & Lowell Railroad and Middlesex Canal; it might well have added to these, the public highways. Of these latter, High and Woburn Streets, as well as the canal and the railroad, passed through the West End. One hundred years before this, Medford citizens had found the most central or convenient location for their meetinghouse and first schoolhouse at the foot of Marm Simond's Hill on High Street, and in 1829 the most convenient situation for the West End schoolhouse was a little way up Woburn Street. For fifty years the canal had its Landing No. 4, with its freight yard, lock and tavern and some two miles of its channel in the West End. The railroad that had succeeded it in popular favor also had stopping places at Symmes' Bridge, Medford Gates, Medford Steps and Willow Bridge, all in the western part of Medford. The Lowell Railroad was opened on June 24, 1835, and is said to have been the first to carry passengers into Boston.

Perhaps it is market day and the stockyards are full of lowing cattle and bleating sheep (just unloaded from the long trains that have come down from New Hampshire), or out on the highway a cloud of dust marks the passing of a drove toward Cambridge or Woburn. All this we see near Willow Bridge. The road to West Cambridge crossed the railway by a wooden bridge of more durable material, but large willow trees along the borders of Winter Brook evidently united with the bridge in suggesting a name for the railway station, which, though still on the Medford side of the line, is now called North Somerville. After passing the cattle yards a road might be seen passing below the track, and on the left toward the setting sun loomed the three-story hotel called the Somerville House. Farther away at the top of Quarry Hill was the old Powder House, a relic of long ago when the Medford people went thither for their grist to be ground—for it was once a windmill tower. Three buildings crowned the top of Walnut Tree Hill, as it was formerly called, the beginning of Tufts College; and the depot across the track, as was also the college site, became known as College Hill.

Bird's-eye view of West Medford, looking from Hillside, 1890s.

Just back from College Hill on the right, sheltered by the trees and hedges, was, and still is, the Stearns residence. With its brick windmill tower it was an attractive sight, to which was added the interest of its connection with another railway, the Underground Railroad of antebellum days.

Passing the old station of Medford Steps with its long stairway—this was on the right hand—and under a bridge now removed, and emerging from the railway cut, the most noticeable object was the First Parish Church, with its several-storied steeple, one of which contained the original town clock presented by Mr. Brooks, while higher up was the bell cast by Paul Revere. At this time it will lack the ornamental finish given later by the Toughs (college boys), that of a black stovepipe hat securely fastened on the three-pronged lightning rod that surmounted the top story of the steeple. Below the meetinghouse the terraced gardens of the Bigelow Estate sloped away from High Street to the mouth of Meetinghouse Brook, while scattered along the road were the old-fashioned houses, some now demolished, among them that of Parson Turell, others remodeled and still remaining.

As the train moved along the view of these was quickly broken by the seamed and scarred promontory of Rock Hill, where once was the home of Nanepashemit, and which commanded a view of the river in either direction. No bridge spanned the river at Auburn Street as now, but the disused canal, innocent of water, was plainly visible before reaching the loop in the river near the mouth of Whitmore Brook, where once a ship was built and launched. Scattered here and there on the gentle slope from High Street to the river, and on the steeper side of Mystic Hill, were some fifty dwellings in 1870, among which the Brooks Schoolhouse stood sharply out as a central figure. These formed the bulk of the West End—the West Medford of 1870.

Across High Street and extending to the shores of Medford Pond, and across the line into Winchester, lay the estate of Mr. Brooks, then as now a place of beauty. At that time two great black walnut trees reared their stately forms skyward, near the old brick wall built by Pomp, the slave; for others beside Colonel Royall had slaves in Medford in the old colonial days.

147

Above: The old brick windmill tower on the Stearns Estate, College Avenue.

Opposite above: The Medford Hillside railroad station, also known as the Medford Steps.

Opposite below: The Brooks School in West Medford, constructed in 1851.

Artist's interpretation of West Medford in the 1870s.

And now having shown you the picture of the West End as the schoolboy saw it, let me say something of the West Medford of the early seventies, as the boy, then a young man, observed it.

The Hillside was unknown, as the term began to be applied some sixteen years later, when the name of Medford Steps was discontinued by the railway company. Only two houses were in that section, and but one, that of Mr. Perkins on Winthrop Street, near the reservoir, was occupied. At

that time (May 1870), there were but eighteen houses west of the railway. Of these eighteen the mansion and farm houses; one house on Canal Street, belonging to Edward Brooks; and two houses owned by the railway company, occupied by Rueben Willey, the station agent, and Daniel Kelley, the flagman, formed a part. On Bower Street were the residences of Horace A. Breed and Henry T. Wood, while near the center of the plain was the dwelling of George Spaulding, which, with its cruciform shape and two-story cupola, was a noticeable object, and sometimes called the steamboat house. The home and two smaller houses of Gilbert Lincoln, and the newly built house of Florist Duane, completed the number not included in the "Smith estate." This composed the territory lying between High Street, the railroad and the river, with a small portion across the track adjoining Canal Street. Some twenty years before it had been laid out in lots, and given the name of "Brooklands," which name, however, had not clung to it. Possibly it blew away in the tornado of August 1851 and like some more tangible objects was lost to general knowledge.

In the seminary building, in what was once known as Everett Hall, Ellis Pitcher kept a grocery; selling out that spring to Sawyer & Parmenter, and they, soon after, to J.E. Ober, who then had a milk route there. No other store of any kind was kept in the West End, but a Mr. Reed, who resided on Allston Street (in the house recently burned), sold dry goods from a wagon and supplied such as came to his house for them.

The post office (established in 1852) was, in '69, kept by Mr. Pitcher, who was in June of '70 succeeded by Mr. Willey; and for ten years the railroad station housed it. Six houses on Woburn Street and six more on Purchase Street formed the outlying district called Brierville. This name must have flown also, as I haven't heard it so called for thirty years.

The rest of the village of '70 was grouped around the Brooks School building, whose ample grounds speak well for the foresight of the town of '67. This portion had been laid out in lots and streets opened in 1845, and in nine years thirty-five dwellings had been erected.

Edward Shaw with his express came not until '71, nor was he located beside Whitmore Brook until five years later. Cunningham's omnibus made no trips to Medford Square, nor did, indeed, until '76, while the bobtail car that succeeded the omnibus would at that day have been deemed a wild enterprise.

Purchase Street (now Winthrop) had been open some twenty-five years, and Woburn Street, once the main road to Boston, was but little used, as the northern travel came not up Marm Simond's Hill. Sugar Loaf Hill had not been cut out so widely, nor yet by the action of the stone-crusher granulated and spread on Medford streets, to sweeten the experiences of travel. Purchase Street was Medford's Via Dolorosa—the way to the almshouse and the silent city of the dead. Mystic Hill, rocky and bare at its top, was beginning to be invaded by dwellers, but they were few and far apart.

In 1872 the organization of churches and the call for more school accommodations became priorities, while a few fires emphasized the need of something more than the ancient hose carriage for protection. New dwellings and churches were built, new residents came, stores were opened and the growing village demanded new avenues of travel. The solid stone piers and abutments of the canal viaduct invited Boston Avenue, while Auburn Street put up a rival claim. The result was that the river was crossed in both places, opening the Hillside and Cotting Street districts. Not a rapid, but a healthy growth has marked the section I have described, so gradually that only the flight of time brings it vividly to notice.

And now let me say in closing, thanking you for your patient hearing and deeming it an honor to have the opportunity of thus presenting this to you, that as I have read these names, I am reminded that while a few still remain, some have removed, while many have joined the great majority and rest from their labors. Each, in his way, bore some part in making the West End what it is.

Originally published in vol. 8, 1905.

MEDFORD HISTORICAL SOCIETY

The Medford Historical Society was incorporated under Massachusetts laws on May 22, 1896. The incorporators were William Cushing Wait, Will C. Eddy, Lorin L. Dame, Mrs. Louise G. DeLong, Miss Helen T. Wild, Miss Eliza M. Gill, Miss Mary E. Sargent, Allston P. Joyce and Charles H. Loomis.

The objects of the society are

> *to collect, preserve, and disseminate the local and general history of Medford and the genealogy of Medford families; to make antiquarian collections; to collect books of general history, genealogy, and biography; and to prepare, or cause to be prepared, from time to time such papers and records relating to these subjects as maybe of general interest to the members.*

Medford is one of the "ancient and honorable" communities of the country. Founded in 1630, its municipal life has been patriotic, dignified and law-abiding, while the family history of many of its citizens is filled with facts and experiences relating to "ye early tymes," which have an irresistible charm for all those who "venerate the historic."

It is a cause for regret that such a society had not been organized many years ago, as doubtless with the breaking up of old families year by year, much of antiquarian interest and value has been scattered, and presumably lost.

Members of the Medford Historical Society, some of them the authors in this book, at the laying of the cornerstone of the Governors Avenue Building, September 30, 1916.

There are many individuals in the community personally interested in historical research, and a suggestion in the local paper, written by Mr. Will C. Eddy, that a historical society be formed found a quick and hearty response from many kindred spirits. Preliminary meetings were held, and organization and incorporation were effected. The charter list contained 132 names.

The society sprang at once into active and aggressive life. In October 1896, it planned and carried to a successful issue a historic festival, happily

named On the Banks of the Mystic, which was conceded to be, as a whole, the finest entertainment ever presented to a Medford audience. The financial results of the festival enabled the society to rent and suitably furnish the quarters now occupied. The house is itself an interesting landmark, having the distinction of a goodly age, and being the birthplace of Lydia Maria (Francis) Child in 1802. A large representation of the society's seal on a wooden tablet designates the building as the headquarters of the Medford Historical Society.

Originally published in vol. 1, 1898.

REMINDERS

Medford was settled in 1630 by followers of John Winthrop.
Enjoyed in her early years the patronage of Matthew Cradock.
During the Revolution her soldiers fought under Washington.
Favored in 1824 with a visit from the noble Lafayette.
On to Lexington through Medford rode gallant Paul Revere.
Recalls with pride the patriotic deeds of Sarah Bradlee Fulton.
Devoted to the memory of her greatest son, John Brooks.

Her history is replete with interest; her record is honorable.
Into the Civil War she sent 769 Union soldiers.
She has ever been foremost in the cause of education.
The keels of Medford-built ships have ploughed every sea.
On the banks of the Mystic shipbuilding flourished seventy years.
Responded with her Minutemen to the call in 1775.
Indian Chief Nanepashemit lived on Rock Hill, 1615.
Cradock House built in 1634 still stands in good condition.
Admitted to have one of the finest high school buildings.
Lydia Maria Child born in house occupied by historical society.

Saw her favorite son seven times governor of Massachusetts.
On College Hill stands Tufts College, opened in August 1855.
City charter adopted 1892; city government organized January 1893.
In natural beauties of woods and hills is well favored.
Enjoys the distinction of being a city of homes.
That because when everyone does something much is accomplished.
You should develop and cherish an interest in Medford history.

Originally published in vol. 1, 1898.

INDEX